Working with Parents

Open University Press
Children With Special Needs Series

Editors

PHILLIP WILLIAMS
Emeritus Professor of Education,
University College of North Wales, Bangor.

PETER YOUNG
Formerly Tutor in the education of children with
learning difficulties, Cambridge Institute of Education;
educational writer, researcher and consultant.

This is a series of short and authoritative introductions for parents, teachers, professionals and anyone concerned with children with special needs. The series will cover the range of physical, sensory, mental, emotional and behavioural difficulties, and the changing needs from infancy to adult life in the family, at school and in society. The authors have been selected for their wide experience and close professional involvement in their particular fields. All have written penetrating and practical books readily accessible to non-specialists.

TITLES IN THE SERIES

Working with Parents

Frameworks for Collaboration

Cliff Cunningham and Hilton Davis

Open University Press
Milton Keynes · Philadelphia

Open University Press
Celtic Court
22 Ballmoor
Buckingham MK18 1XW
and
1900 Frost Road, Suite 101
Bristol, PA 19007, USA

First published 1985
Reprinted 1988, 1991

Copyright © 1985 Cliff Cunningham and Hilton Davis

British Library Cataloguing in Publication Data
Cunningham, Cliff
　　Working with parents: frameworks for collaboration.
　　——(Children with special needs)
　　1. Professional employees　2. Parents
　　3. Interpersonal relations
　　I. Title　II. Davis, Hilton　III. Series
　　331.7'12　　HD8038.A1

　　ISBN 0–335–15036–5
　　ISBN 0–335–15035–7 Pbk

Library of Congress Cataloging Publication Data
Cunningham, Cliff
　　Working with parents.

　　(Children with special needs series)
　　Bibliography: p.
　　Includes index.
　　1. Parents of handicapped children　2. Parent-
student counselor relationships　3. Personal construct
theory.　I. Davis, Hilton　II. Title　III. Series
　　HQ759.913.C86　1985　362.8'2　85-13777

　　ISBN 0–335–15036–5
　　ISBN 0–335–15035–7 Pbk

Typeset by The Bath Press, Avon
Printed in Great Britain by
Thomson Litho Ltd, East Kilbride, Scotland

To our wives and children.

Contents

Acknowledgements

It has been possible to write this book only because of our experiences of working with families of children with special needs. Without their help we would have learned very little.

We are also enormously grateful to Mrs Susan Wells for her work in typing the many drafts of the book.

Series Editors' Preface

Throughout the world today, medical, educational and other specialists are urged to work with the parents and families of children with special needs. Cliff Cunningham and Hilton Davis address themselves to the central problem of what to say to these professionals which will help them to work more harmoniously, more perceptively and more effectively with parents. They write for members of a wide variety of callings, for therapists, for nurses, for doctors as well as for teachers and other educationalists. Traditionally, but with some notable exceptions, specialists were trained in a way which assumed they were equipped to work with their young patients or pupils and that this fitted them to work with the parents too. The powerful influence of the medicine-man was transmuted into the doctor's bedside manner, the psychiatrist's couch wreathed in cigar smoke, and the psychologist's or teacher's rapport – a French borrowing with a frisson of the séance about it. Together with the assumptions of omniscience and dedication, these were often deemed all that was necessary to deliver diagnosis, prognosis and programmes to parents.

Now the scenario, if not the actors, has changed. Legally and professionally parents are seen as participating partners in the identification, assessment and meeting of special needs. Parents are accurate assessors and predictors, a resource, providers, client–consumers of a service delivery system. They are also managers, governors, tax-payers, accounters of professional accountability and potential litigants. Parents are thus as multi-faceted and are no more stereotypical or homogeneous than their children. Working with them, co-operating with them, demands that we perceive them clearly and deeply. But, and here's the rub, the specialists, therapists, teachers, advisors, social and welfare workers are a multi-disciplinary and heterogeneous group, too. Moreover, much of the really effective training appropriate to interaction between professionals and between professional and parents, must be live and participatory. Sensitivity training, role-play, simulation, life-skills and group-therapy skills cannot properly be developed by reading about them. And, without falling into generalities appropriate only to the lowest common denominator, the problem is to identify what can be said to specialists which is relevant, rigorous and rugged.

What makes this book a valuable contribution to its comparatively new and certainly most demanding subject, is that the authors, from their own experience working in the field with other professionals, have identified a unifying but flexible framework which is itself scientific and interdisciplinary without being eclectic or flaccidly effete. In George Kelly's Personal Construct Theory (PCT) they have a base from which, as they convincingly demonstrate and illustrate with case-studies, to illuminate our perceptions of professional, parental and patient roles. Kelly saw man as a scientist 'seeking freedom amid swirling events', each one of us constructing theories based upon our experiences of reality and anticipating events accordingly. His description of the ways in which we use our constructs nicely illustrates labelling and categorization. Kelly's pre-emptive construct postulates, for instance, that, 'He's blind so what do you expect!' The constellatory construct, however, fixes the elements within the stereotype's realm: 'He's blind, carries a white stick, tunes pianos and is led around by a guide dog'. Only the propositional construct is without implications attached to the construct: 'He's an internationally famous composer and pianist named George Shearing, who happens to be blind'.

It is the scientific nature of PCT, akin to Popper's concept of science, as a line of argument with its own integrated language, which makes it so adaptable and so powerful a tool for professionals from different disciplines. It is Kelly's view of the therapist–client situation which makes it so appropriate for working with parents: 'Neither is the boss, nor are they merely well-bred neighbours who keep their distance from unpleasant affairs. It is, as far as they are able to make it so, a partnership'. Our authors, in their application of PCT to working with parents, might well have adapted Kelly's first principle of self-characterization: 'If you don't know what is wrong with the parents, ask them, they *may* tell you'. With Kelly they are able to view other therapies from other disciplines as techniques which, if they are likely to be efficacious, will be used within the context of the client experimenting in his own right rather than being manipulated as a 'subject'.

Cliff Cunningham and Hilton Davis look at the many ways in which parents today participate in intervention programmes, or may be given support. Whether it be Home-Start, Honeylands, Portage, home–school links, family and other therapies, or parent contact groups, their key concept of counselling parents is clearly demonstrated. They see the family as an open system, accessible to and susceptible to professional and community support, and parents as partners to whom it is essential that we listen. This, combined with their interdisciplinary approach and their open-mindedness, enables them to demonstrate the use of Personal Construct Theory as a framework through which specialists may use their professional knowledge and skills with wisdom in partnership with participating parents.

Phillip Williams
Peter Young

CHAPTER 1

Working with Parents

Parents are experts too. Help should begin with an understanding of what they believe, expect and need. This is the foundation for all efforts to help their child. If they (professionals) listened to parents, trusting them to be competent and capable, instead of giving instructions all the time, they would be more useful. It is easier to receive, when you are giving. (Parent's comment)

Many changes have occurred in recent years in relation to children with special needs. The term, special needs itself, for example, reflects major conceptual change. Children are no longer categorized into groups such as the maladjusted, the mentally retarded, the physically handicapped, those with visual or auditory impairment and specific learning difficulties. Instead, an attempt is made to determine the needs of specific children in relation to their particular circumstances. Special needs are defined in terms of what the child requires beyond those normally required for all children. For example, they include special educational provision, housing, mobility, finance, physiotherapy, diet, speech therapy, medical treatment and so on.

Other changes include the movement towards community care as opposed to residential placement, with the implication that families will be more involved. Associated with this is a move towards wider integration of children with disabilities into the community, as well as an emphasis on early identification and provision. There has also been in many areas a rapid increase in knowledge which is of potential benefit to those people interacting directly with the child. This broadening conception of special needs and community care has resulted in an expansion of professionals involved in the field and more frequent interaction between parents and professionals. Most parents of children with special needs will come into contact with general practitioners, medical or surgical specialists, clinical medical officers, health visitors, nurses, teachers and educational psychologists. Depending upon the nature of the child's difficulties, they may also see physiotherapists, social workers, clinical psychologists, peripatetic teachers, dieticians, genetic counsellors, audiologists and so on.

Together with this increasing contact with professionals, parents are demanding more say in medical, social and educational issues which affect their children. This reflects a more general change in society towards a desire for democratic control and individual self help. This is particularly true for parents of children with special needs where evolution of services has largely resulted from parental pressure. Such changes acknowledge the importance of parent–professional collaboration, the very basis of which is mutual sharing of relevant knowledge and skills considered to be of benefit to the family and child.

It is our intention in this book to examine the nature of this collaboration. The justification for collaboration has been made on a number of grounds ranging from the moral to the practical. The former includes the recognition of the rights and responsibilities of parents with respect to what happens to their child and the latter accepts the notion that parents and families have major influences on the child's development.

Parental Rights and Responsibilities

Parents are the legal guardians of their children and as such are ultimately responsible for them in all ways. Professional involvement does not negate this responsibility, except in extreme circumstances where such rights are removed by legal action. Above all, parents are the primary advocate for the child. No other person, professional or otherwise, can function like a parent in this respect. Parents have the right to make both reasonable and unreasonable demands on behalf of their child. In fact, the parent has the responsibility to involve professionals when required and therefore has the right to expect consideration and an active attempt by the professional to communicate honestly and accurately. To do so requires a close, trusting and co-operative relationship.

Benefits for Child and Family

The influences of the family and social context upon the child are widely recognized and will be discussed later. The implication of this is that professionals need to work more closely with families. In this way, not only may professionals help the child directly, they may also assist the family generally and help the family help their child.

Information

Children with special needs are not a homogeneous group and neither are their families. It is impossible to make broad generalized statements about them that will have assured accuracy in many cases. For example, it is not true to say that Down's Syndrome children are all more friendly than other groups of children or that all children suffering birth hypoxia will show specific symptoms subsequently. For the professional, therefore, there is not available a generalized body of knowledge which will allow precise judgements about how to help such children. Predictions about the usefulness of treatment or educational methods and their outcomes are particularly difficult. If professionals also try to see the whole child in relation to the family and social circumstances, then considerable information is needed.

It is necessary, therefore, to understand each child individually and this requires extensive observation of the child on different occasions and in various situations as a preliminary to intervention. Since parents are usually with their child most frequently and in the widest range of contexts, they are obviously well equipped to provide much relevant information. Consequently, they have an important role to play in, for example, assessment procedures. Similarly, the parent will be the major source of information about how the family works, its resources and needs. The professional requires access to this to ensure effective help for the family as a whole.

Remedial Action

Certainly in the early years, if not later, parents are in most continuous contact with their children, and have considerable influence over them, being actively engaged in teaching. They are more likely to be the primary attachment figures and are the most obvious models for the child's learning. They regulate much of the stimulation available to the child and are in the most important position to control the learning opportunities available to the child. With a child who has special needs, they may require a variety of help to be most effective. Therefore, it is both economic and efficient for professionals to share their skills with the parent. It is argued that this should provide better generalization of learning to the natural environment and is more likely to ensure maintenance of newly learned skills. Equally important is that such help may prevent unnecessary difficulties for the child and the rest of the family from developing.

The difficulties of a child with special needs may have disturbing effects upon the parents and other children. Such disturbance may in turn disturb the help they can give to the child. Consequently, even though the job specification of the professional is to work with the child, the goals can only be obtained by a broader involvement with the parents.

If one accepts these arguments then one fundamental requirement that is made of the professional is to consult parents and to find out what they feel they need. In fact, they have stated their views for many years, as is seen in this eloquently phrased example by Mrs Murray:

> The greatest single need of parents of mentally retarded children is constructive professional counselling at various stages in the child's life which will enable the parents to find answers to their own problems to a reasonably satisfactory degree. (Murray, 1959).

Since listening to what parents have to say is a reasonable starting point in working with them, then a consideration of their criticisms of available services is appropriate at this point.

Main Categories of Criticism

Communication
This is perhaps the most frequent source of criticism. Complaints tend to involve:

(a)   insufficient information,
(b)   inaccurate information,
(c)   excessive information at any one time,
(d)   information that is not understood because of the use of technical language or poor presentation.

Such criticisms apply to all forms of communication, including those in writing. They arise because of professional failure to appreciate the parents' current knowledge or emotional state, or their ability to understand and remember what is being said.

Perceived Feelings

Parents often complain about the professional's lack of warmth, concern, interest and compassion. These criticisms can be summarized as a failure to express empathy and respect for the parent and child. This is conveyed when the professional rushes or dominates the interaction, provides no privacy, discourages questions and fails to listen. Similar feelings are conveyed by the quality of facilities and the venue of the interactions (e.g. having consultations in school or hospital corridors). This can be illustrated by the following parent's comment:

> The first assessment. Well! There were so many different people there . . . It was frightening. Professional people talking at you and discussing your child as if you were not there.

Such comments suggest a failure by professionals to view their own activities from the perspective of parents.

Competence

Parents complain about professional competence, such as the teacher's failure to control a class or the physician's incorrect diagnosis or prognosis. Whilst parents are not necessarily in the best position to make such judgements, their trust in professional competence is of primary importance. The ability of professionals to interact well is of little consequence if they fail to demonstrate technical competence.

Resource Availability

A common criticism refers to the absence of necessary services or their insufficiency. Parents are, therefore, either not given the help they want, or they are given a minimum of help involving long delays.

Service Accessibility

Although adequate services may be provided, parents frequently complain about their inability to use them. They may not be advertized adequately and there may have been a failure to take account of geographical problems (e.g. the location of a clinic in relation to the home), time factors (e.g. appointments at times when father is at work) or other practical difficulties (e.g. arrangements for other children whilst attending an appointment).

Organization

Parents complain that the services are disorganized in a variety of ways ranging from punctuality of appointment keeping to poorly organized meetings or old and inadequate buildings. All such complaints reflect upon the attitude of the professional and perhaps indicate to the parents that they are being devalued.

Co-ordination

Parents are frequently expected to answer all the same questions each time they meet a different professional. They may also often act as the messenger of information from one professional to another. Going over old ground can be emotionally upsetting, as can the responsibility of accurately conveying information between professionals. Parents also often complain about receiving conflicting advice from different professionals. Such criticisms are a reflection of the lack of co-ordination between different aspects of the services.

Continuity

Since children with special needs have long-term problems, continuity of services is vital. Nevertheless, complaints are made about the failure to see the same professional on repeated visits and that resources may be available at certain times but not at others. For example, at the birth of a damaged child enormous help may be provided only until the child is discharged from hospital. More help may then be provided during the school years with inadequate facilities once again when the child passes school age.

Effectiveness

Finally it is not uncommon for parents to say that professionals do not listen to what they have to say about their needs and the services to meet them. This implies a lack of commitment to the notion of evaluation and accountability to parents.

Implications for Practice

These complaints have a number of implications for the improvement of services generally. One set of implications concerns the organization and availability of services, which are largely dependent upon policy and finance, and beyond the scope of this book.

The second set concern the personal qualities of all professionals when interacting with parents. It is with these that we are concerned. It is our contention that in addition to their specific training, all professionals require the skills and knowledge to establish effective relationships with parents in order that their specific expertise can be implemented fully. This is true for the health visitor advising the parents on how to feed the child, the teacher discussing the aims of her programme for the child, the paediatrician giving a diagnosis, or the G.P. prescribing a drug. To all these interactions we will give the term, *counselling*.

We are not, therefore, using the term counselling to refer to a specialist technique. If any two people are talking and one asks advice of the other or tells the other of some current difficulty which they cannot resolve, the other person is placed in the potential position of becoming a counsellor. If this person then relates how a similar problem was resolved, suggests alternative explanations, or, by listening and sharing their own feelings helps to reduce the problem, he/she is counselling. Thus it is one person's perception that another may have the competence and willingness to help that initially characterizes a counselling situation. If the other responds with the intention of trying to help, the counselling process has begun.

Clearly, when a person consults a professional, competence can rightly be assumed and constructive action expected. The professional has to respond with the intention of helping. When consulted, professionals may provide answers to the parents' stated problem. They may often only ask questions which they, as professionals, feel are required on the basis of the parents' initial statements. However, what is really required is to help the person to explore and identify the main features of the problem and to set up a negotiated set of options to provide solutions.

A major characteristic of this is that the person seeking help wishes in some way to make changes. For parents these changes usually concern some benefit for the child. Often this will involve changes in the parent or family and these are more likely to occur within a mutually trusting and respectful relationship between parent and professional and they will take time.

It follows from what we have said, that all professionals are already involved in the business of counselling. Since the skills of this are the social skills of interacting and communicating with others, we are all potentially reasonably skilled because we have had practice in them from birth. Our contention is, however, that we can all improve considerably by attending to and practising these behaviours specifically and by making explicit the models or frameworks of understanding that guide our behaviour. Our intention in this book, therefore, is to help to elaborate necessary frameworks, as we perceive them, and to begin to describe the relevant skills. The reader will, however, have to obtain the appropriate training for these independently, since they are skills and as such must be practised.

Frameworks

We believe that the elaboration of these frameworks is important because they guide our actions. We carry in our heads ideas and images which we use as reference points and templates to make sense of ourselves and our world. Heifetz stated this clearly when he said:

> Professionals cannot work truly effectively with parents unless they are acutely aware of their own conceptual framework, . . .

He went on immediately to add that they must also:

> . . . understand the broad outline and finer detail or each parent's framework and begin to anticipate the manner in which the two frameworks interact as the parent–professional relationship evolves. (Heifetz, 1980, p. 350)

Though frequently implicit, these frameworks can be made explicit, and as such, may become models which can direct our behaviour more objectively and help to initiate change. By 'model' we refer to a conceptual framework or theory. For example, we could explain a child's aggression in terms of a 'hydraulic' model, as though tension builds up like water behind a dam and explodes violently when it reaches a certain level, the point at which the dam overflows or crumbles. To be useful, a model should make existing knowledge more meaningful. It should also be testable, in that it should allow reliable predictions to be made and evaluated. The usefulness of the model will be reflected by the outcome of the evaluation.

To illustrate, John Bowlby (1951) constructed a model which predicted that a child, in the first years of life, must have a loving and unbroken relationship with its mother in order for normal emotional development to occur. If we adopted such a model, we would be led to make a number of predictions, which would influence our behaviour in relation to families. For example, we would ensure that children remained with their mother in the event of marital breakdown. We would avoid taking a child into hospital in a way that separated the child and mother and we would frown upon mothers leaving their children in order to go to work.

Whilst such predictions may be accurate or inaccurate, they can be tested, as has occurred since the maternal deprivation model was first proposed. Although it has been shown to be misleading in many respects, it has generated important research which has demonstrated the possibility of multiple caregivers, the irrelevance of the sex of the caregiver or the blood relationship and the importance of other factors such as good relations between various members of the family (Rutter, 1972).

Thus models are not absolute and can be changed. They are a *guide* to our behaviour. They enable us to make the most informed guess or prediction possible at the time and therefore to take the most reasonable course of action. Thus, the book is largely concerned with discussing frameworks and models to do with the parent–professional relationship and the counselling process.

It is initially essential for professionals to ask how they view the way they should work with parents and hence, the basis of their relationship. This is therefore discussed in the following chapter and inevitably requires some consideration of parent and professional roles. Once decisions have been made about a model of how to work with parents, professionals will need a psychological framework to understand how individuals behave and how they change. This is discussed in Chapter 3, where we describe what is for us a useful framework, Personal Construct Theory (Kelly, 1955). To work with parents and families one must have some conception about parenting and how families work. In Chapters 4 and 5 we discuss some views on this and the effects of having a child with special needs on both parents and families. In Chapter 6 we present a framework to make sense of the process of counselling and we describe the associated skills needed by professionals. Chapter 7 attempts to bring together the principles outlined in earlier chapters through a brief overview of current ways of working with parents.

CHAPTER 2

Parent–Professional Relationships

In this chapter we are going to consider the relationship between parents and professionals. This is to a large extent influenced by professional behaviour which is partly determined by the way professionals view their role in relation to parents. Our aim, therefore, is to explore the often implicit models that professionals have about the relationship. To do this we will abstract and contrast three models that are evident in current practices. For convenience we will call these the Expert, Transplant and Consumer models. Of course, in reality no two professionals will operate identical models nor will any specific professional be entirely consistent in using a particular model. Our purpose is to simplify what is very complex in order to illustrate a range of possible frameworks that professionals use, often unconsciously.

The Expert Model

Professionals use this model if they view themselves as having total expertise in relation to the parent. Here essentially professionals take total control and make all the decisions. They select the information that they think is relevant to the parent and likewise, elicit only that information that they feel is required. In this model the parental role is only considered in so far as it is necessary to carry out instructions given by professionals in relation to their objectives. Consideration of parental views and feelings, the need for a mutual relationship and negotiation, the sharing of information are all given low priority. Because these are regarded as irrelevant to the solution of the problem, one finds parents expected to wait outside treatment or assessment rooms, and as late as the early 1970s, open visiting for parents in hospitals was the exception and not the rule.

Given that there is no attempt in this approach to involve the parents, it is not surprising that it is frequently found that parents are reluctant to question the professional, that there is distorted understanding, high levels of dissatisfaction and non-compliance (Ley, 1982). Another difficulty is that this approach may foster dependency in the parent rather than reinforcing feelings of competence. Such dependency will have the effects of increasing demand for the professional's services and decreasing the parents' ability to help the child because of reduced self-reliance and feelings of relative incompetence in relation to the professional. As one mother said:

> How can I teach him anything, when the teacher has to have all those years of training and qualifications.

Such parental expectations can result in a demand for professionals to act out the expert model even at the expense of over-generalizing their range of competence. This is reflected, for example, in the reluctance of many professionals to admit that they do not know answers to certain questions. Indeed, an advantage of this model is that it protects the professional by providing self-confidence and status, and it prevents outside threat. In so doing, it enables the professional to continue to work in situations that have considerable uncertainty. There can be few professionals that have not at some time retreated into this expert mode of action when stressed or threatened; hiding behind jargon or statements about an area being too complex to explain or arrogant assertions of status.

Finally, a major danger of this model is that in not eliciting the parental perceptions or alternative views, the professional may consider the child from one point of view (e.g. learning ability or symptoms) and thereby neglect him/her as a whole being within a general physical and social network. This may lead to missing important problems within the child, and to neglecting problems that the parents experience. It is also likely to increase parental dissatisfaction by failing to meet their expectations.

The Transplant Model

Professionals are using this model when they view themselves as having expertise, but also recognize the advantage of the parent as a resource. They recognize that part of this expertise, previously the prerogative of the professional, is usefully uprooted and 'transplanted' into the care of the parents, where it might, so to speak, grow and be fruitful. This model has been seen increasingly in recent years in all professions and is well documented. For example, physiotherapists provide exercises for parents to use with children with cerebral palsy; home visitors train parents in behavioural and educational methods to work with their children with mental handicap (e.g. O'Dell, 1974; Dessent, 1984).

Since the professional role is seen as transplanting skills they retain control of decision making, as in the expert model. Overtly or covertly, it is the professional who selects objectives, treatments and teaching methods. Nevertheless, in this model parents are perceived as willing to help their children, appropriately placed to do so and in need of the skills that will enable the child to progress. They are, therefore, viewed as relevant, and they become an extension of the services. This recognition of the relative competence of the parents is likely to reinforce their self-confidence and adjustment, as is their active involvement in helping their child.

Because parents become partly responsible for assessment and the communication of results to the professional, there is less likelihood of aspects of the problem being neglected. Equally, the professional is dependent upon feedback from the parent and is therefore more likely to view the child as a whole, within the context of the family. This model also endorses the view that the continuity of contact of child and parent allows for more consistency of learning opportunities, and increased likelihood of the generalization and maintenance of progress.

To apply this model, additional skills are required by the professional. These are essentially the ability to instruct and maintain an ongoing positive relationship with the parents. This change in emphasis is likely to improve professional–parent communication in general and is therefore likely to decrease dissatisfaction, misunderstanding and non-compliance.

An important problem that can occur, however, is for professionals to assume homogeneity amongst the parents with whom they work. There is a real danger of ignoring the individuality of families, with their own skills, characteristics, anxieties and values. It is possible that they will expect all parents to comply automatically with their instructions and to be competent in the skills taught. This is also more likely to foster dependency upon the professional. Of course, parents may not share the aims and values of the professional; they may not have the resources to carry out the tasks required; the family may be much too disorganized to be able to respond in the way the professional requires. If this occurs, excessive demands may be made, and as a result hostility may occur. Such hostility may be mutual and therefore devastating in terms of the provision of necessary help. The professional must be extremely careful to tailor methods specifically to the family so that they are not overburdened, for example, or so that other children in the family are not neglected. Underlying these dangers is the failure to make explicit the need for open discussion, negotiation and shared decision-making.

The Consumer Model

Professionals using this model view the parent as a consumer of their services. This means that the parent is seen as having the right to decide and select what they believe is appropriate for their consumption. Within the parent—professional relationship decision making is ultimately in the parent's control. The role of the professional is to provide the parent with the range of options and the necessary information from which to select. In this model, the professional respects the parents and acknowledges their competence and expertise in knowing more about their total situation than anyone else.

As in the previous model, the professional acts as a consultant and instructor, but in this model, since the decision making lies ultimately with the parent, negotiation within the context of a mutually respecting relationship is the foundation. By negotiation we mean a process by which the professional and parent attempt to reach mutually acceptable agreements. The responsibility of the professional is to listen and understand the parents' views, aims, expectations, current situation and resources, to provide alternatives to be evaluated and to help the parents to reach realistic and effective decisions. Obviously this cannot happen unless the interaction is set within the context of an honest relationship in which there is a free flow of information between them. In much current parental involvement the flow of information is largely one-way, from the professional to the parent, from the school to the home. Arguing that the parent is ultimately responsible does not divest professionals of all responsibility. Their responsibility is to negotiate all stages of the decision making process. Clearly the concept of negotiation is, in fact, a central aspect of the counselling process discussed in Chapter 1.

An advantage of this model is that the professional is less likely to treat parents as an homogenous group or to impose only one approach as a solution to family needs. What is required is flexibility to meet individual child and family needs. This is achieved in this model, since there is less chance of assuming adequacy, justification and effectiveness of the services provided. There automatically exists an in-built evaluation process, because the emphasis is upon understanding the needs of the consumer and negotiation with them. This enables the needs of the family to be expressed and an assessment to be made of the extent to which they are met.

The danger of fostering dependency and eroding the parents' feelings of self-confidence and self-competence is reduced, because one can only operate this model by treating them as competent. This recognizes not only their rights, but their expertise and they are accorded an equivalent status in the relationship. Compared with the previous models the balance of power between the parents and professional is more equal. One implication of this is that professional power is not entirely determined by their professional status, but by their effectiveness in establishing the negotiating processes and helping to find solutions. It follows that the professional in this model is more vulnerable. The defences of superiority, indispensibility and infallibility are not so easily maintained. Their expertise is much more open to scrutiny. Furthermore, in sharing skills with the parent, professionals may feel they are giving away parts of what determined their original professional status. This, however, may be offset if they acknowledge that the ability to negotiate and to impart their skills to parents is a vital aspect of their professionalism.

As noted previously, a potential obstacle to this approach is the tendency for parents to expect omniscience and omnipotence from professionals. Although such feelings can initially help to engender trust and relieve anxiety, it is unlikely that any professional can match this, given the complexity of the problems of children with special needs. Both parents and professionals may have to make considerable changes, especially in their views of each other, in order to operate the model. However, what is important about this model is that by making negotiation a key principle, expectations are inevitably elicited, explored and become part of an explicit contract. Since the model emphasizes open, accurate and two-way communication, the professional and parent will be more aware of each other's expectations. The close correspondence between satisfaction and expectations leads to the prediction that operating within this model will result in high levels of satisfaction and compliance.

Implications for Parent–Professional Collaboration

The advantages of parent–professional collaboration were discussed in Chapter 1, where it was argued that the nature of the relationship is largely determined by the model (explicit or implicit) that the parent or the professional has of it. The three models described largely differ in the extent to which they acknowledge the need for, and seek to establish, a collaborative relationship. The major differences relate to the acknowledgement of the expertise, responsibilities and rights of each (i.e. the parent and professional) to benefit the child.

In the expert model the parent is seen as being responsible for seeking out professional help with the professional taking control thereafter and making the main decisions with minimal negotiation. Little priority, therefore, is given to providing the time and skills for negotiation.

On the other hand, the consumer model acknowledges the parental responsibilities to the child, their expertise and their right to some control over decision making. To do this, priority must be given to the necessary resources and skills needed to establish negotiated agreements. This cannot happen unless professionals have the necessary training and resources.

The nature of the collaboration, however, will also vary according to the area of need. The teacher required to develop ongoing parental involvement for children with special needs will clearly need different resources from those of the orthodontist. The orthodontist will have the main expertise in diagnosing some of the child's dental needs and advising on treatment, and will be less dependent upon information from the parents. The parents will, however, be largely responsible for explaining to the child what is going to happen and why, alleviating any of the child's fears, preparing the child for visits and negotiating with the child any restrictions to activities during the course of treatment. To be successful in this role, they will need some basic information about the treatment. The professional will need to provide this and also in many cases elicit information about the child's fears. If time is limited alternative forms of communication, such as illustrated pamphlets, assist the process. *These not only provide the information but convey to the parent the professional's view of the relationship.*

This collaborative approach has been referred to as a partnership (Mittler & Mittler, 1982; Mittler & McConachie, 1983; Pugh, 1982). The term partnership acknowledges the sharing of expertise in order to achieve some common purpose. The expert model could not be described as a partnership. There is an implicit contractual agreement of sorts, in that the parent expects the expert to solve the problem. The responsibility for success or failure is largely in the hands of the expert. The parent plays a peripheral role largely dependent upon the professional. This may satisfy both parties and certainly many parents are very happy for the professional to be mainly responsible for the treatment or teaching of their child. However, they generally wish to have some control over the major aims or objectives for their child. Of course, if the treatment or teaching fails, the parent's peripheral role may make them feel less directly responsible. They can blame the school or doctor for the lack of success rather than their own actions. Although they may feel less responsible, most would probably find this cold comfort.

The transplant model offers a partnership but places the parent in the role of junior partner, dependent on and supervised by the professional. By being directly involved in the treatment or teaching the parent takes on some responsibility for the success or failure of the approach. The danger in the case of failure is that the parents may not have the degree of detachment that the professional has, and so find failure harder to bear.

In constrast, the consumer model is based upon the assumption that the parent has considerable knowledge of the family needs and resources and that the relationship should share this within a partnership. Clearly, what is recognized is the different but complementary roles and expertise of the parent and professional. The notion of equality does not apply as the partnership assumes that each partner will have different roles and expertise, which will be applied for different needs and at different times. Thus, the dominance of any member will vary.

The professional may negotiate to take over the major responsibility for the child or decision-making when parents are under such pressure that this responsibility would merely increase stress. Ideally, the process of negotiation should lead to mutually agreed solutions in which the parents have executive control over major decisions. This should reduce the likelihood of failure due to incompatibility between family resources and professional advice. In situations, however, where treatments have failed, then the parent has to accept some responsibility, but it is shared with the professional. Because of the immense variability among children with special needs, predictions about the success of approaches are difficult and failure to achieve an objective is not unusual. It is essential, therefore, that the partnership honestly shares both information and uncertainty.

This model is obviously more time-consuming and demands

a far wider range of professional resources than the expert model. A partnership is a contractual arrangement, and as such each partner has at least minimal expectations of the other. It is important that these expectations are seen as reasonable by the partners and, therefore, they should be made explicit.

Minimal Expectations

The professional can expect the parents to provide certain basic living conditions for their child. They should provide adequate nutrition and physical comfort and take reasonable steps to prevent illness and injury. Additionally, it is the parents' responsibility to provide an environment in which the child's development is not impaired, as far as can be judged. These are minimum requirements upon which parents usually substantially improve. They commonly provide a warm, loving and stable relationship and an environment which would optimize the development of the child. Developing or maintaining this may be seen as the primary aim of parent counselling. Where parents fail to meet these minimum responsibilities then the notion of a partnership may be less applicable, as in the case where the child is being physically injured or where parents are unable to form a loving relationship. However, using counselling to establish an eventual partnership may be an appropriate aim.

Similarly, there must be minimal expectations that the parents have of professionals. Firstly, and most obviously, they should expect the professionals to be competent by virtue of their training, knowledge and experience. Perhaps more important, however, is that this competence be perceived by the parents in all ways; for example, in the advice that is given, in organization and in the analysis and attempted solutions to problems.

Professionals should be expected to care for and value both the child and the parents. The respect professionals might expect from parents should be reciprocated. This will be demonstrated in all the dealings professionals have with the parents. Caring professionals should also be expected to show compassion and a willingness to try to understand the parents' views. By compassion is not meant pity, which is devaluing. It means the willingness to help even when no solutions are obvious, when professionals feel least confidence in their skills and most vulnerable, when success and job satisfaction are not obvious. Whether or not the attempt is successful, there should be the willingness to try to share their feelings and ideas.

The parent can expect the professional to have the necessary social skills to communicate effectively and counsel skilfully. In all this, the professional must recognize that the parents are the legal guardians of their children and as such are ultimately responsible for them in all respects. Professional involvement does not negate this responsibility, and so parents can expect that professionals will acknowledge this by recognizing their right to make decisions on behalf of their child.

Parent and Professional Roles

Since the partnership is largely based upon the complementarity of differences between parent and professional, it is essential to recognize the differences (Katz, 1980; Newson & Newson, 1976).

Firstly, the functions of parents are broader and more diffuse than those of professionals. Most professionals dealing with the child will tend to have a reasonably specific set of aims or areas of interest set within relatively defined limits. Thus the speech therapist will largely be concerned with the child's language or speech difficulties, whereas this may be one of many areas of concern for the parent.

Secondly, the parents will have more interactions with their child in a wider range of situations than the professional. Consequently, it is likely that the parent can offer the professional a broader picture of the child in terms of, for example, the extent to which the child's behaviour generalizes to different situations. Most teachers are well aware of the change in their constructions of a child when together on a trip or holiday. Parents may tell psychologists or doctors that the child's performance in the context of a development test is far more limited than in other contexts.

Thirdly, a major difference is that parents are more emotionally involved with the child than professionals. This means that parents will have more intense reactions and feelings to the total spectrum of the child's behaviour than professionals.

This will include joy, pride, love, as well as anger, anxiety and fear. Emotional differences clearly effect the style of interaction between child and adult. The teacher may happily deal with high failure rates and repeated presentations in a learning task, whereas each failure and presentation incrementally stresses the parent. Hope, pride and fear for the future may make parents impatient. They want the child to achieve the goal and so focus more on the goal attainment than on the process of achieving it. This may be why siblings are often so much better, according to parents, at teaching the child with learning difficulties. They may be less concerned about the goal and more interested in the ongoing inter-action.

The strong emotional attachment between the child and the parents is also likely to make their interpretations and constructions less objective than those of the professional. One function of professionals is to bring objectivity to the partnership. They try to act in as rational a manner as possible, carefully reasoning what should be done. This detachment or objectivity is an attribute for professionals, but its development in the parent to the same extent cannot be expected. Extreme objectivity or detachment in parents may be construed by the child as calculating and cool. Parents' reactions are marked by variety and spontaneity. They interact in a confident, unself-conscious manner. The interaction is important for its own sake with enjoyment on both sides, rather than for some specific external purpose. On the other hand, professionals strive to make their interactions as purposeful as possible. Therefore professionals must be careful to ensure that the contrast, variety and spontaneity of the parent–child relationship is not damaged as a result of professionals implicitly or explicitly imposing their style of interaction. Similarly, one must be careful not to restrict the opportunism that characterizes a range of interactions between parents and children. As Sondra Diamond (1981) said about her parents:

> I would be off in a euphoric state, drawing, or coloring . . . , and as often as not it would be turned into an occupational therapy session. 'You're not holding the scissors right,' 'Sit up straight so your curvature doesn't get worse.'

This ended with her tirade of:

> I'm just a kid! You can't therapise me all the time! I get enough therapy in school every day! I don't think about my handicap all the time like you do!

Finally, parents are responsible for their child, treating him or her as someone special, whilst professionals are responsible for many children and are expected to avoid partiality. Parents, there-fore, are likely to be the most vigorous advocates on behalf of the child, and as such legitimately make demands that may appear unreasonable and impractical from the professional viewpoint. Unless this distinction is acknowledged and negotiated, it can lead to conflict. It is therefore reasonable to raise the general question about the extent to which parents can be expected to merge professional and parental skills without inhibiting their enjoyment of their children.

Practical Exercise

Professional Assumption Grid

Whatever model a given professional adopts, it is important that they know the kinds of assumptions that are being made. To help uncover such assumptions, the reader is asked to do the task set out below.

   Draw a grid of squares with 10 columns and 18 rows as shown in Figure 1. At the top of the first column put the name of a child with whom you have worked and about whom you feel able to answer questions. Put the name of a second child at the head of the next column and so on across the columns. It does not matter if you cannot supply the full ten names. Each row of the grid will be used to answer specific questions about each of these children and their families. There are 18 questions and they are as follows:

   1.   Have I met the family?
   2.   Do I consider the child in the context of his/her family?
   3.   Do I have regular, two-way communication with the family?
   4.   Do I respect and value the child as a person?
   5.   Do I respect and value the family?
   6.   Do I feel the family has strengths to help the child?
   7.   Have I identified the parent's abilities and resources?
   8.   Do I always act as honestly as possible?
   9.   Do I give them choices about what to do?
   10. Do I listen to them?
   11. Have I identified their aims?
   12. Do I negotiate with them?
   13. Do I adjust according to the joint conclusions?
   14. Do I assume they have some responsibility for what I do for their child?
   15. Do I assume I have to earn their respect?
   16. Do I make the assumption that we might disagree about what is important?
   17. Do I believe they can change?
   18. Have I tried to identify the parent's perceptions of their child?

Number the rows from 1 to 18 to represent each of the questions. Begin with row one and answer question one for each of the children. Put a figure 1 in the appropriate box if your answer is 'Yes' or a '0' if the answer is 'No'. Do the same for each of the questions.

		JOHN	KAREN	KATE	JAMIE	INGA	JUSEF	ANGIE	SAM	PETER	JANE	
Q1	Met Family?	1	0	0	1	0	0	0	1	0	0	3
Q2	Consider context?	1	0	0	1	0	0	0	1	0	0	3
Q3	Two-way communication?	1	0	0	0	0	0	0	0	0	0	1
Q4	Respect & Value child?	1	1	1	1	1	1	1	1	1	0	9
Q5	Respect & value family?	1	0	0	1	0	0	0	0	0	0	2
Q6	Family strengths?	1	0	0	1	1	0	0	0	0	1	4
Q7	Abilities & resources?	1	0	0	1	0	0	0	0	0	0	2
Q8	Honesty?	1	1	1	0	0	0	1	0	0	0	4
Q9	Provide choices?	1	0	0	0	0	0	0	0	0	0	1
Q10	Listen to them?	1	0	0	1	0	0	0	0	0	0	2
Q11	Identified aims?	1	0	0	0	0	0	0	1	0	0	2
Q12	Negotiate?	1	0	0	0	0	0	0	0	0	0	1
Q13	Adjust to conclusions?	1	0	0	0	0	0	0	0	0	0	1
Q14	Responsibility?	1	0	0	1	0	0	0	0	0	0	2
Q15	Earn respect?	0	0	0	0	0	0	0	0	0	0	0
Q16	Disagree?	1	0	0	1	0	0	1	0	1	0	4
Q17	Assume change?	1	0	0	1	0	0	1	0	1	0	4
Q18	Parents perceptions?	1	0	0	1	0	0	0	1	0	0	3
		17	2	2	11	2	1	4	5	3	1	48

Figure 1   Example of a Professional Assumption Grid

When you have finished, total the scores for each row and each column separately. The total of all the columns should equal the total of all the rows. This grand total may indicate roughly the extent to which you are considering parents and to what extent you are operating a family orientated consumer model. A high total score will indicate a generalized use of a consumer model. A low score on the other hand may indicate an expert model.

It may be, of course, that you behave and perceive in different ways according to the family. It may been enlightening, therefore, to look at the totals for each column separately. By looking at the totals for each row more useful information may be available. From the example in Figure 1, we might infer that the person in general does not use a consumer–partnership model. The grand total is only 48, when it could potentially be as much as 180. However, by looking at the column totals the first column is very high compared to the others, which indicates that this family is given full consideration and respect. This family, in fact, lived in the same neighbourhood as the professional and there were frequent contacts, shared social activities and common interests. In considering the row totals, row 4, for example, stands out by its extremeness. This suggests that the professional has a 'child-focused' approach.

CHAPTER 3

Understanding Individuals

To work with parents and their children, we must know how we view them and ourselves. How do we *make sense of them* and *anticipate* what we should do in our relationship with them? In other words what frameworks or models do we have in order to interpret and understand our own behaviour, that of the parent and child and our interactions with them? A variety of frameworks can be used. For example, in intellectual impairment it has been common to employ what might be called a medical model. The child is seen in terms of a number of symptoms (e.g. spasticity, seizures, etc.) which together form a syndrome (e.g. cerebral palsy). This in turn is seen as the result of physical pathology (e.g. damage to brain tissue) which arises because of a specific aetiology (e.g. oxygen starvation at birth). Such a model is attractive, since it guides the search for physical treatment and possibly preventive measures. On the other hand, it does little to enable predictions about psychological and remedial educational measures. The danger is that if the parent or professional uses organic causes or damage (i.e. pathology) as the dominant model for making sense of most of the child's behaviour, this is likely to result in further handicap as it will predict that there is nothing that can be done. When this happens one's prediction is fulfilled because one does nothing; it is a self-fulfilling prophecy, with handicap resulting from depriving the child of the necessary help for his or her development. The pathological model, therefore, becomes pathological in a further sense of adding to, or at least failing to remedy, the existing problem.

Another example of a common model is the psychometric view of the child as someone with a low I.Q. It has been an important

23

approach in the past and has been useful as the broadest first step to assessment. Nevertheless, like the medical model it is pathological in classifying individuals in terms of what they cannot do and not facilitating predictions to be made about providing effective help for the family and child. The move to concepts like 'special needs' is a good example of a change from a pathological model to one which is more constructive in potentially suggesting necessary remedial actions.

These models attempt to make sense of the child, but do not enable us to understand parents' behaviour or our own in relation to them. There are, however, a range of psychological models that attempt this. Selecting from the array of possibilities can be bewildering, and often ultimately depends upon the compatibility between the model under consideration and one's current personal views and needs. For example, there are social learning theories which interpret people's actions in terms of their perception of rewards (Rotter, Chance & Phares, 1972). There are psychodynamic theories which are more concerned with unconscious control of behaviour (Freud, 1974). Recently, interest has developed in the model of Transactional Analysis, particularly for those concerned with counselling, because it seeks to explain relationships in terms of transactions between people (Woollams & Brown, 1979).

The assumption we have been making throughout the book is that all people are attempting to construct models of the events confronting them in everyday living. Therefore one can ask the question, 'How do people construct these models?'; 'How does a parent make sense of their child with a handicap?'; 'How does the child seek to understand the professional?'. Because we believe that collaboration with parents demands a negotiated understanding of their perceptions (their models), we have found that the Theory of Personal Constructs as described by Kelly (1955) both matches and complements the consumer model of working with parents. For a concise description and review of this approach see Bannister & Fransella (1980). The theory has been considered in relation to education generally by Pope & Keen (1981) and in **relation to mental handicap by Davis & Cunningham (1985).**

Foremost, Personal Construct Theory is based on the premise that the essential characteristic of people is that they construct models in order to anticipate events. Essentially then, all people are viewed as scientists and, therefore, it is a very *respectful* model in that it applies equally to the behaviour of the scientist, professional, parent or child. An additional advantage is that the theory is explicitly stated in a systematic way that is easily communicated.

Consequently it offers the possibility for a common model shared across different disciplines in the field of special needs which should facilitate communication and transdisciplinary development.

It is important to note that this theory is not being discussed in order to exclude alternative models necessarily. It is not, for example, intended to replace a behavioural approach, which has been the most dominant model in the area of special needs in recent years. The behavioural model has been and remains extremely useful (Yule & Carr, 1980; Wheldall & Merrett, 1984) particularly in relation to producing changes in children's behaviour. In fact, it is quite possible that the outcomes of using a construct theory or behavioural approach will be the same on many occasions in terms of how to analyse problem situations and how to remedy them. The behavioural approach is, in fact, a set of constructs that enable one to make sense of a situation in a particular and potentially useful way. However, there are alternative ways of making sense of the same situation and what construct theory does is to make explicit the process of making sense (i.e. anticipating) of the events and the need to consider alternatives.

The Theory of Personal Constructs

The basic statement of the theory is very succinct and is in the form of a fundamental postulate and 11 corollaries, as follows:

Fundamental Postulate: A person's processes are psychologically channelized by the ways in which he anticipates events.

Construction Corollary: A person anticipates events by construing their replications.

Individuality Corollary: Persons differ from each other in their constructions of events.

Organization Corollary: Each person characteristically evolves for his own convenience in anticipating events, a construction system embracing ordinal relationships between constructs.

Dichotomy Corollary: A person's construction system is composed of a finite number of dichotomous constructs.

Choice Corollary: A person chooses for himself that alternative in a dichotomized construct through which he anticipates the greater possibility for extension and definition of his system.

Range Corollary: A construct is convenient for the anticipation of a finite range of events only.

Experience Corollary: A person's construction system varies as he successively construes the replications of events.

Modulation Corollary: The variation in a person's construction system is limited by the permeability of the constructs within whose range of convenience the variants lie.

Fragmentation Corollary: A person may successively employ a variety of construction subsystems which are inferentially incompatible with each other.

Commonality Corollary: To the extent that one person employs a construction of experience which is similar to that employed by another, his psychological processes are similar to those of the other person.

Sociality Corollary: To the extent that one person construes the construction processes of another, he may play a role in a social process involving the other person.

The basic assumption of the model is that all people are concerned to anticipate what happens to them and around them. Their principal need is to make sense of the world, to be able to make accurate predictions, so that they can adjust adequately to their situation. To make the world meaningful in this way, each person constructs in her/his head, a model of events. The word construct is used to imply that the model is not god-given or a simple replica of reality; the individual builds the model on the basis of her/his experience, any part of which can be perceived or interpreted in a variety of different ways. For example, the pen used to write these words can be variously seen as 'something to chew whilst thinking', 'something to stir the coffee', 'something mightier than the sword' or 'something to throw at the cat'.

The model built by the individual guides her/his behaviour. It enables the person to interpret an event such as a situation or the behaviour of another person. On the basis of the interpretations he/she makes, appropriate actions can be taken. Whether the interpretation is accurate or not, the individual who sees a situation as dangerous, is likely to act in order to reduce the danger. The mother who sees her child as naughty will behave in ways intended to stop the perceived naughtiness. Her interpretation is real to her, even if others would disagree with her view of the child's behaviour. One parent's perception of what constitutes a behaviour problem may differ from another parent's view, yet it is equally real at the time. For example, how many nights and for how long in the night would a child have to wake up for it to be called a problem? Therefore, if we are to work in a respectful partnership with parents we have to accept the reality of their interpretations and not oppose or ignore them.

Since events in the world are complex, one might expect the

model that is constructed to reflect this complexity. In order to understand it, therefore, Kelly suggested that we view the model as a set of discriminations that the person can make. Each discrimination Kelly called a construct. For example, discriminating between people who are honest as opposed to dishonest, is a construct. Similarly, discriminating between black and white, adult and child, or, as we attempted in Chapter 2, professional and parents, are examples of three separate constructs. The model, therefore, can be seen as a set of constructs. It is a structure composed of a large number of constructs, each of which need not be conscious or expressable verbally, and will apply to a limited range of events. For example, the construct, 'honest–dishonest', may be used to apply to oneself and other people, but not to pens.

At this point you might have thought that the term 'construct' is the same as, for example, an idea or an attitude. In a way it is, but it is not simply an additional concept; it is used as a replacement. There are a multitude of terms in everyday language that refer to very similar events 'in the mind'. For example, those we have just mentioned, as well as values, knowledge, cognitions, rules, perceptions and so on. By using a single word (i.e. construct) we simplify this complexity. For example, we might ask a mother how she views her child. She may say she likes him very much but thinks he has quite severe learning problems. We could debate whether such an answer reflects the mother's feeling, values, attitudes or perceptions, with little profit. In this model, all we need to do is to say this is how she construes the child. The result is that we have a parsimonious model that does not require us to differentiate and define all these alternative and overlapping notions.

It is assumed, therefore, that in our heads we have a set of constructs. Kelly viewed this set as an organized system and not a haphazard group. He assumed that constructs related to each other in various ways. For example, a decision to lend money to someone will depend not only upon your construct of them as 'honest–dishonest', but also upon the constructs of 'forgetful–unforgetful', 'seen frequently–rarely seen', 'have money to spare–have insufficient' and so on. Similarly, a diagnosis of mental handicap is a construct which implies a number of other constructs such as 'of low I.Q.', as opposed to at least 'average I.Q.', 'socially inept vs. socially skilled', 'needing supervision vs. independent' and so on. Meaning and resulting behaviour is therefore derived not from single constructs, but from a number of constructs in interaction.

The fact that individuals are all very different in their reactions may be explained in terms of their different construct systems. People will differ in the number of their constructs, the content of them and the way in which they are organized. Nevertheless, individuals will show some similarities in that there are constructs that are shared. Within a culture, the fact that we all share common assumptions about the world, facilitates interaction. We share constructs about how to behave towards others, about what is right and wrong, and therefore, we are able to anticipate what is appropriate behaviour in social situations. In general, therefore, it is both our shared and unique constructs of other people that determine how we interact with them. This statement, therefore, is at the foundation of such notions as partnership, collaboration and empathy.

Of course, the construct system is not fixed, but is evolving all the time. We respond to a given situation in terms of the way we construe it. Any construct may or may not be accurate. If it is, then the construct is unlikely to change. If, on the other hand, our anticipation is found to be wrong, or invalid, then the construct is likely to change. For example, the health visitor may view a mother as having adjusted well to the diagnosis of heart disease in her child, but this changes dramatically when subsequently the mother indicates that she is expecting her child to engage in strenuous physical exercise. This invalidates the initial construct and she has to reconstrue the mother differently. Similarly, a mother who had always construed herself as incapable of controlling her child, would have to change her view of herself if she found that the use of the approaches advised by the psychologist enabled her to get her child to do what she said.

Although Kelly used words like anxiety, fear, and guilt, he used them in ways that are somewhat different from the usual rather vague meanings that are assigned to them. We will explore this aspect of the theory more fully in the next chapter. Briefly, however, he defined emotions in relation to the process of change, *as the awareness of significant or imminent changes in the construct system.* For example, anxiety is viewed as the person's awareness that the events with which she/he is confronted lie mainly outside the realm of his/her construct system. In effect, the person is unable to understand what is happening in that there are no constructs available to anticipate the particular situation. As a result he/she either has to develop totally new constructs to understand the events or has to change existing constructs in ways that allow some sense to be made. This relates as easily to the situation of parents taking their first baby home from hospital after the birth, as to the situation experienced when we think of dying. In either case, we face unknown situations.

Implications for Working with Parents

With the intention of clarifying these somewhat abstract notions, we should now like to consider the implications of the model for professionals working with parents and children. For convenience, we will look at parents and children separately, then consider their relationship, followed by the implications for the professional.

Parents

Like all people, parents throughout their lives develop a construct system to make sense of the world. Once they decide to have children, then a part of that system must become elaborated for the specific purpose of anticipating the behaviour of their children and their own behaviour in relation to them. This part of the construct system will be built up to an extent during pregnancy. It may have its origins in the experiences parents had in their own childhood and experiences of children known to them, but attention becomes focused upon the activities of children and their caretakers in the months preceding the birth. One mother's comments about her first pregnancy was: 'I hadn't noticed it before, but suddenly every woman I saw was pregnant and there were babies everywhere.'

The initial, rather cautious way in which parents handle their first child is a clear expression of their lack of knowledge, their unelaborated construct system, which subsequently develops very quickly and evolves to match the changes that occur in the child. For example, when the baby is a few weeks old, the parents' statement that 'We have to walk around with him to get him to sleep' is a construct of one aspect of the child. It is the parents' way of anticipating what to do with the child, and it will change as the baby matures and they find other ways to get the child to sleep. Again, regardless of its accuracy, the view that 'She must be teething' is used to explain all kinds of short-term changes in routine and irritability in the child.

The constructs used by parents give meaning to their baby's behaviour and allow meaningful interaction, even if the reality is somewhat at odds. For example, a spontaneous and random vocalization of a newborn may be construed (i.e. interpreted) as 'he is talking to me'. A fleeting facial change may be seen as a smile and interpreted as reflecting the baby's feelings; for example, the construct 'she likes you'. At this stage the accuracy of the constructs may be unimportant. What is probably more significant is that the parents make interpretations which lead them to assume that the child intends to communicate with them and therefore lead them to interact socially with the child, which may be seen as an important precondition of subsequent developmental progress.

If you *listen* to parents you can see just how often they express their explanations/constructions. In fact, everything they do and say is a manifestation of their constructs. For example, a rather complex set of constructs is evident in the following attempt of one father to describe his son to another adult: 'He goes wild occasionally. I don't understand it really and my reaction is to get angry, but I feel I shouldn't. He seems to do it when other people are around and when he's tired and when there's been a change in his life. It also seems to precede a leap in his development . . .' The constant attempt to understand is further illustrated by a mother who described her child's imitation of the behaviour of a more aggressive child as 'an attempt to appease her (the other child); to become so much like her that she will be safe'. Such an explanation does justice to a psychoanalyst, even though expressed by a mother without access to such professional training. Even a child's silence and absence is made meaningful and may be interpreted differently, as in the case of two mothers who were sitting in one room with their children elsewhere, when one suddenly became worried and said, 'I can't hear them. What are they up to?' and the other calmly replied, 'They're quiet, they must be O.K.'

Although we have given examples of verbal expressions of constructs, parents do not necessarily use constructs consciously, nor may they always be able to put them into words. For example, if you asked a mother why she did something to her child (e.g. give him/her a particular toy) she may not be able to say. When asked why she kept picking up her son, one mother replied that she did not know. The questioner suggested that it was because she felt he was being naughty and she accepted this explanation at first. On reflection, however, she argued that it was her view of the child as unhappy that provoked her behaviour, since the child was only naughty when he was unhappy. Whatever is the truth of the situation, this example perhaps well illustrates that there are alternative ways of construing the same event and that the constructs are not necessarily conscious or explicit, but are an automatic part of our existence.

What we have said here applies to all parents, whether their children have special needs or not. The only difference is that parents of children with special needs have to face at least one major crisis (i.e. the diagnosis), which may disrupt their ability to anticipate the behaviour and the development of the child. As we shall see, this ability is further hampered by the fact that their child is very different from other children. Most other children around them will be unlikely to have, for example, motor impairment, specific learning problems or generalized developmental delay. This means that the parents will be unable to look at other children and use this information to make sense of the behaviour of their own child.

The most significant crisis, perhaps the first of many, occurs around the point of diagnosis. If the child has just been born and has, for example, Down's Syndrome, then suddenly the parents are confronted with a situation that is usually far outside the range of their constructs. This is an example of massive anxiety, as defined earlier. They will not have anticipated having a child with special needs, so their predictions about the child based upon their construct system evolving during the pregnancy will be immediately invalidated. Secondly, in most instances they will know little or nothing about such children, in terms of causes, present characteristics or future development. If we assume, as we have, that it is a prime motive of people to be able to understand and anticipate, then parents in this situation must be incredibly vulnerable. They will be in a state of considerable confusion and uncertainty. The description of them as in a stage of numbness and shock is apt, since they are unlikely to know how to react, given they have no basis for grasping what has occurred.

People do not, however, remain unable to predict, they set about rebuilding a framework to enable them to understand. Following the shock, parents begin to ask questions. This is the first strategy in gaining information for reconstruction. They need to know the causes of the disorder, what can be done about it, and what the future will hold. Not surprisingly, it is the uncertainty of the future that is most difficult for both the professional and the parents. In working with families at this time, we frequently listen to them questioning their own ability to cope individually, or questioning the strength of their marital relationship and the effects upon their other children.

The same process can be seen not only in asking overt questions, but in all their reactions. Parents may consider killing the child or leaving it in the institution. These should be seen not as mere pathological reactions to stress, but as strategies serving an important purpose. They are strategies that allow the situation to be explored in order to aid the reconstruction process. They are potentially beneficial and should not be discouraged. Anger directed at the maternity and paediatric staff should be accepted as one way of trying to understand. It allows one possible set of causes to be explored. Even denial of the problem may be, at least temporarily, adaptive, in enabling the parents to retain the model they had before the crisis, thus allowing space to consider the situation when they have the strength. Though this is an extreme case, the same may occur with any children. For example, a father who was suddenly informed that his nine-year-old child, who attended the local primary school, required remedial reading said, 'I was totally shocked. They (the teachers) didn't think about him the way I did. They knew he was different to other kids and we had no indication. I got very angry with the teacher about it. I kept questioning her and I didn't believe what she said. I was so upset. I upset my son and I spent hours discussing it with my wife trying to understand.'

Gradually, most parents will reorientate themselves in terms of being able to understand their situation sufficiently well that they can set about the process of adapting to it. At this stage they will have developed a new construct system allowing them to adjust to daily life with the child, and even to attempt remedial action. A more extensive discussion of the reactions to the diagnosis of an impairment and the process of adjustment can be found in the next chapter. Of course, their adaptation can never be absolute, but it is relative to their situation at the time. Readjustment must occur as the child does or does not develop and as new events, such as the diagnosis of further impairments or even the recognition of new gifts occur. Even events such as beginning or leaving school require changes in the model the parents have developed. For example, one set of loving, competent parents had enormous difficulties adjusting to their highly intelligent teenage son with severe cerebral palsy going to boarding school. Their problem can be understood in terms of being unable to change their model of their son as dependent upon them, and themselves as his caretakers. They construed themselves as letting him down, because they had always promised him that he would stay at home. Amid the many other reasons for their difficulties was their inability to know whether their actions had been for the benefit or detriment of their son.

The diagnosis of handicap at a significant time after birth is in principle no different from that already discussed. As before, the parental model may be shattered and a different construct system has to be rebuilt. However, a major difference is that the construct system about the well child will have been more elaborated and fixed by experience and may therefore be much more resistant to change. In one family referred for help more than two years after their child had suffered severe brain damage at 5 years of age, the mother described herself as having two daughters; the healthy, bonny child before the accident and the disturbed, embarrassing, severely retarded child following it. She talked of her desperate need to tell strangers who saw the child, what she had been like originally. The former system or model remained intact and was a constant influence upon this mother. In depressed periods she would shut herself away in her bed and comfort herself by vivid recall of her 'original' daughter.

The Child

Regardless of age or severe impairment, this model views the child as a person actively trying to make sense of his/her world. In so doing, it takes the child seriously, accords the child respect and avoids simply placing a label on the child. The model is not pathological in the sense discussed earlier; it does not focus upon the negative and by doing so further confound the problem. The danger with diagnosis in a medical sense is that a label, such as mental handicap or cerebral palsy, somehow fixes all the characteristics of the child that we might expect to find. In Construct Theory terms this is called either pre-emptive or constellatory construing. The child is either 'mentally handicapped' and nothing else, or is 'mentally handicapped' and, therefore, 'of low I.Q.', 'socially maladapted' and 'ineducable'. This process of constellatory construing is well exemplified with reference to children with epilepsy. Although this is a construct that says only that the child has periodic manifestations of seizures of the central nervous system, such children were also likely to be seen as having an epileptic personality. The symptom of epilepsy would lead to them being seen as, for example, aggressive, slow and irritable, even though there was no evidence for the suggested personality profile. The tendency to think in such ways relates more to attempting neat and tidy pigeonholing, or to use Kelly's words, cramming 'a whole, live, struggling client into a nosological category', rather than trying to discover educational methods or 'lines of movement open to a person'.

Regardless of the severity and causes of children's impairments, they are not pathological specimens. They are human beings elaborating a system of constructs to help them make sense of and anticipate the events they experience. It may be that their impairment impedes the process, with the result that they are able to make fewer discriminations, may be less accurate in judging, may be slower to see that a prediction is invalid and slower to change when they have. Nevertheless, they make the attempt. The child with a specific learning impairment may struggle to make sense of, for example, the written word. The child who is blind may struggle to develop an alternative to a visual model of the world. A severely intellectually impaired child may struggle with most things. All of them, however, can do nothing but to try to understand.

This view of children has direct implications for educational strategies. The first is that we might change the emphasis in the curriculum. Instead of deciding what we should attempt to teach on the basis of developmental milestones, we can look at the child as an individual who has a set of ways of understanding the world and a set of related behaviours for acting upon it. To progress, therefore, we would need to understand what constructs the child has in order to try to communicate more effectively with and to attempt to help him/her to develop further constructs that may be of more value. Where a child cannot talk, the constructions that she/he uses have to be inferred on the basis of non-verbal behaviour. That this is a difficult task is shown by the example of parents who wanted to reduce the frequency in their Down's Syndrome child of what they had learned from professionals to call a stereotypy (a repetitive stereotyped response with little obvious purpose). They referred to a pattern of behaviour which involved finger-wagging and hand-flapping. By asking what they thought was the function of this behaviour for the child, and by observing when and how often it happened, the parents came to the conclusion that the behaviour was a way of expressing enjoyment. The result was that they were able to use the behaviour themselves to communicate some of their own feelings to the child, rather than attempting to eliminate the response as they had originally intended.

Although it is difficult, this approach makes explicit the aim of trying to understand the world from the point of view of the child. As is shown in the above example, this means trying to share the constructs the child uses, rather than necessarily imposing a set of constructs upon the child. Once the child's own constructs are clearer, the parent or professional is in a better position to anticipate ways of helping to develop them. If, for example, a severely intellectually impaired child has very few constructs, we might expect him/her to fail to discriminate between different situations and therefore to use the same behaviour in a far too general way. To effect a change, it might be important not to increase the environmental stimulation, as parents and professionals may naturally expect, but to reduce it, by simplifying the environment and consistently marking the significance of the important aspects. For example, rather than talking constantly to the child, it may be advisable to talk less frequently, more simply and at particular points in the interaction.

In the past, it has often been assumed that within the constraints of the genetic endowment of the child, it is the behaviour of the parent that in some way moulds the development of the child. There have been a number of approaches in developmental psychology that have had this implicit assumption. In contrast, the more recent view is that parents and infants both affect each other. That is to say, the parent acts towards the child and therefore may influence the child's development, but each child is different from birth and her/his behaviour influences the way in which the parent behaves. Their relationship must be seen as a closely related system such that development cannot be understood by considering the behaviour of the child or parent in isolation. This kind of approach has lead to the conclusion that successful development is a mutual process. For example, when they interact, they take turns in talking and listening, their behaviour is closely timed to that of the other and this is the result of carefully monitoring the behaviour of the other.

To this picture we need to add a dimension concerned with the ways in which each individual in the interaction construes the behaviour of the other. We might, therefore, usefully try to understand interaction in terms of the model presented in Figure 2. This shows that an action performed by the child is an event that can be construed by the parent, whose behaviour is then regulated by the construction placed upon the child's act. In turn, the behaviour of the parent is observed by the child and construed in a way that produces a further action on the child's part, and the cycle continues, until one or other directs her/his attention elsewhere. Of course, this in itself will be construed by the other with relevant behaviour resulting. This is based upon Kelly's Sociality Corollary that says *we can only play a role in relation to others to the extent that we can construe the constructions of the other*. It is only by observing the behaviour of the other, however, that we can make judgements about how they construe.

Of course, it is not only her construction of the child's behaviour that influences a mother. As shown in Figure 3, her behaviour

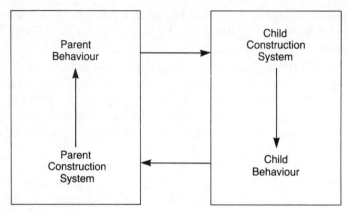

Figure 2   The Cycle of Parent–Child Interaction

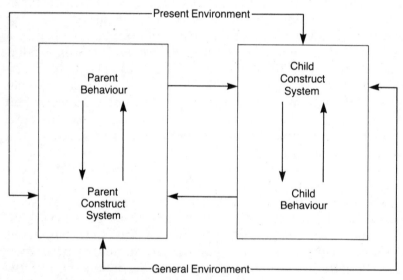

Figure 3   The Interaction Cycle and Other Influences

will also be influenced by (a) how she construes her own behaviour
(e.g. 'I shouldn't have done that'; 'It will spoil her'); (b) what
she construes as valuable (e.g. 'I want him to be polite'); (c) how
she construes the present context, including the presence of other
people (e.g. 'My mother will think I'm being soft'); (d) the ways
she construes all aspects of her environment (e.g. 'If we had more
money, a better house, . . .'). In a similar way, the child's behaviour
may also be influenced.

To illustrate the usefulness of this model to the professional, we will give a number of examples of how the model could be used to make sense of the way in which specific problems may have arisen and subsequently developed. It is important to realize that no matter where in the cycle shown in Figure 2 a problem arises, it will have implications for all other aspects of the diagram. We will begin with an example of a problem in which it was probably the child's behaviour specifically that initiated the cycle of changes.

A mother of an 18 month old boy was referred because of the child's temper tantrums. The psychologist listened to long out-pourings which centred around the mother's unhappiness and inadequacy as a parent to make her son happy. She felt her son hated her and she had begun to hate him. After careful observation of the child's emotional expressions, the parents reported back excitedly that nothing seemed to make him smile and that close contact made him annoyed. What is more, they felt that this had always been the same. They then elaborated the following explanation. The child rarely showed positive emotion (i.e. child's behaviour) and mother saw this as unhappiness (i.e. mother's construction). She, therefore, tried harder to comfort him (i.e. mother's behaviour). This was presumably seen by the child as aversive (i.e. child's construction), since he only cried and struggled (i.e. child's behaviour). Consequently, in time mother began to see herself as disliked by her child and therefore an inadequate parent (i.e. mother's construction) and she began to attend to her son only when she had to (i.e. mother's behaviour).

Difficulties may also result because a child has problems construing events in a meaningful way. For example, a child with intellectual impairment will have difficulty in elaborating an adequate construct system. Since he/she will therefore be unable to anticipate the behaviour of his/her parents, his/her behaviour may not synchronize with that of the parents. They may explicitly or implicitly construe the child as 'incapable of behaving otherwise' or 'unable to know better' or 'its not her/his fault', and this will influence their behaviour. For example, they may take over from the child as in the case of not only asking the child a question, but also supplying the answer. The finding that parents and professionals increase the rate of their speech to handicapped children may illustrate this tendency. Parents may also construe themselves as 'not understanding' or 'inadequate' or in any number of other ways, but whatever they believe, it will influence their behaviour towards the child, who will again have difficulty in understanding. In such circumstances it is very easy to see how the synchrony of the interaction may be difficult to sustain and may become a one-sided task with the child contributing little.

Of course problems may arise, not because of factors in the child, but because of the constructs or behaviour of the parents. For example, one couple began to worry that their healthy son had suffered brain damage in a fall. They began to look for signs of it in whatever he did; their model of the child somehow began to have the construct of 'damaged' as central to their perceptions of him. Almost everything the child did had possible significance. If he slept excessively or did not sleep, these were clear signs of a problem. His increasing resentment was seen as related to disinhibition because of brain damage. In fact, because of their construction, they became very anxious and overtly controlling in their behaviour to him. Not surprisingly, the child construed this as interference and responded by trying to distance himself. Again we see the knock-on effect through the cycle of interaction. The effects were quickly reversed when the parents were helped to reconstrue their situation. The medical records of the original accident were acquired and shown to the parents. These documented the fact that there had been no head injury. The parents were given information about head injuries and saw that, even if their child had hit his head, little damage would have been likely as he suffered no unconsciousness. Such information removed their anxieties with the result that they reduced the degree to which they tried to control him, and this, in turn, led to the child being less distant and so on.

These relatively extreme examples serve to illustrate what may occur to a lesser extent when parents, because of love for their child, with or without special needs, become preoccupied with the unfairness, the dangers or the possible suffering in their child's world. Naturally, they may try to regulate events to prevent physical or emotional suffering in the child. What might be called overprotectiveness is perhaps the parents' attempts to suffer *for* the child rather than *with* the child. In many families, the parents may need to realize that they cannot prevent all possible upsets for their children and that it is not advisable to try, since children will learn from a degree of adversity.

The model presented here not only has value in understanding causal sequences, but more important is of value in suggesting remedial action. For example, a mother who construed her child as 'attention-seeking' and 'deliberately getting at me' when the child persistently interfered with hot pans on the stove, was rightly concerned about this very dangerous behaviour in her eight year old severely intellectually impaired daughter. Her interpretations were not at all unreasonable, since the child's grinning face, when told off, could easily be seen as 'daring mother to interfere'. However, with professional help, the mother began to consider alternative explanations, one of which was that her daughter was trying to be helpful. This led her to observe her daughter more carefully in a number of household situations. As a result, the child was seen to show the same kind of behaviour, in trying to hold on to the vacuum cleaner and the iron whilst grinning in precisely the same way. In consequence the mother changed her construction of her daughter's behaviour from 'attention-seeking' to 'wanting to help', and was able to alter her kitchen to give the child her own stove on top of the tumble dryer. The immediate effect of this was to stop the child's exposure to the dangers of boiling water, because she was too preoccupied with her own cooking! The role of the professional in this case was not to supply an expert opinion as an explanation, but to prompt the mother to consider alternative explanations (i.e. constructions) which she was able to test by making appropriate observations. The evaluation of such observations led to her reconstruing the behaviour of her daughter.

The model may even be useful in analysing and further understanding behavioural methods in ways that increase their successful application. Behaviour modification can be seen as a closed construct system which leads us to view behaviour in terms of constructs like, for example, stimuli and responses, antecedents and consequences of responses and reinforcement (i.e. events that strengthen preceding responses). Such a system of constructs allows us to anticipate that if reinforcement is an immediate consequence of a response, the response will be more likely to reccur in the same situation. For example, if we praise a naughty child warmly for obeying a command, he/she will be more likely to obey a subsequent order. Although this may work well, it may not be the most useful explanation, to say that the child became more obedient because she/he was reinforced. In terms of Personal Construct Theory, it might be that the parent, by praising each obedient response, became more consistent in behaviour with the result that the child noticed the consistency and construed it was worth his while to do what was required and therefore obeyed. The process of the interaction cycle continues, however, because the parent may then reconstrue him/herself as more 'effective' with his/her child and may construe the child in more positive ways. Consequently, the parent may change his/her behaviour in several ways such as becoming more positive, more relaxed, more tolerant, as well as more consistent.

The Professional

Just as we can see parent–child interaction in the way illustrated in Figures 2 and 3, so can we see the interaction between the parent and the professional. The behaviour of each will depend upon the behaviour of the other and the models they build up for making sense of each other. Therefore, it is important to ask how parents construe professionals. Obviously this process begins with the parents' construction of the label attached to the professional (e.g. social worker, speech therapist, etc.). As we noted in the first chapter, their constructions of the function of these disciplines will lead them to anticipate what help they can get. It is essential, therefore, that the professionals find out how parents construe them and their role in initial interactions. Subsequently, it is the constructions placed upon the professional's behaviour by the parent, and not just the behaviour *per se*, that is the effective ingredient in the relationship.

We believe that the model outlined in this chapter has relevance to the professional, in helping to make some sense of what is a most complex set of circumstances and events. It is very easy to be overcome by the wealth of information presented by families, especially when they present problems, for example, of a psychological and social nature, that may not be central to the technical skills of, for instance, the teacher, physiotherapist or physician. However, the model may also help professionals to understand their own reactions. Professionals should always try to be in touch with their own perceptions and emotions about the parent–professional interaction in order to behave appropriately and effectively. It is not uncommon for parents to behave in ways that make professionals feel threatened, by, for example, questioning their ability. Defensiveness is a natural response, yet it is of little value in these circumstances. However, if professionals have a prior awareness and understanding of what makes them defensive and how they react, then they can contain these feelings better, and even use them to good effect. For example, on one occasion it was very productive to tell a father that everything he did and said made the psychologist feel useless and that perhaps that was why the family had never obtained consistent help from any of the several professionals who had tried.

The model has been criticized, usually at an academic level, in a number of ways. It has been said that it assumes that people are more rational than they are, or that the emotional component of behaviour is ignored in this approach. Some have criticized it, because it denies unconscious determinants of behaviour in the psychoanalytic sense, and others, because it deals with events in people's heads or minds, that cannot be objectively studied. In general, many of these comments relate to the fact that the Theory of Personal Constructs does not fit into the general mould of other psychological theories, yet seems to be all embracing.

Whatever the academic criticism and regardless of the model's unmeasurable absolute validity we put it forward because of its potential usefulness. Each reader should consider it carefully in terms of whether it makes sense to them and most important, whether it helps them to make sense of their professional position in relation to the people they are trying to help. Thus the model is an attempt to impose a measure of rationality. It will not answer all the possible questions related to the understanding of individual behaviour, but it may answer some and clarify others. Like all frameworks, it is necessary to use the model practically in order to understand it and evaluate it and therefore we have included suggestions in the practical exercise for beginning this process.

Practical Exercise

The Child Characterization Sketch

The following exercises serve to illustrate (a) the theories/constructs that parents have about their children and (b) the problem in eliciting, recognizing and understanding them.

A. The following passage was one parent's answer to the question, 'Would you please try to describe the character and personality of your child as fully as you can?':

> He's a very active child, but you don't know how he'll be. One day he's happy, the next he's completely different: He won't sit down for long; he won't concentrate on anything; he'll bang his head and have fits of temper for reasons I don't understand. Sometimes it's because he can't get what he wants. He's very miserable at times, really miserable. He cries a lot. He doesn't sleep. He doesn't like people interfering. If you try to play, he'll get really upset.

This is, in fact, a free expression of at least some of the constructs that she uses, in relation to her child.

1. Can you look at the passage carefully and list separate constructs without reading further for the moment?
2. To do what you have just done, we use the rules listed below. Apply them to the Child Characterization Sketch

and see what constructs you get now.

- (a) List in the mother's words each separate characteristic mentioned.
- (b) Do not include characteristics that are repeated, using the same or very similar wording.
- (c) List separately descriptions that you think may have the same meaning, but are expressed in different words.
- (d) List mother's descriptions of herself separately.
- (e) List as separate constructs all descriptions of place or context (e.g. 'At home'; 'When shopping'; 'If I say no'.)

3. Compare your results with our results obtained for the same Sketch. (i) 'a very active child' – rule a; (ii) 'don't know how he'll be' – rule a; (iii) 'happy' – rule a; (iv) 'completely different' – rule a; (v) 'won't sit down for long' – rule a; (vi) 'won't concentrate' – rule a; (vii) 'bang his head' – rule a; (viii) 'have fits of temper' – rule a; (ix) 'for reasons I don't understand' – rule a or d; (x) 'can't get what he wants' – rule a; (xi) 'very miserable' – rule a, with second use of 'miserable' omitted under rule b; (xii) 'cries a lot' – rule c; (xiii) 'doesn't sleep' – rule a; (xiv) 'doesn't play with other children' – rule a; (xv) 'a loner' – rule c; (xvi) 'doesn't like people interfering' – rule a; (xvii) 'If you try to play' – rule e; (xviii) 'he'll get really upset' – rule a.

4. Each of these statements represents the way the mother sees her child, the way she construes her child, the aspects of him that she can discriminate. Each statement represents one pole of a bipolar construct (e.g. 'a very active child' represents one pole of a construct such as 'active–passive' or 'active–inactive').

5. Before reading further, decide what conclusions you could draw from this mother's list? What predictions might you make about this child and this mother?

6. You might conclude that the mother has described the child almost entirely in negative terms. She described what he does not and cannot do, and what he does that is naughty. Perhaps the only positive construct relates to being sometimes 'happy'. She is describing what amounts to a child who has severe behavioural difficulties, is generally unhappy and socially isolated. To make the situation even more difficult, the mother has hinted that the behaviour is unpredictable (i.e. 'you don't know how he'll be'; 'for reasons I don't understand') and incomprehensible. Con-

sequently, it may be anticipated that the mother is being confronted with an extremely stressful situation which may tax her attachment to the child severely with the possibility of rejection of the child and breakdown of their relationship. In fact this child was actually taken into care some months after this description was recorded.

B. 1. Try to arrange to see a friend or a friendly parent of a child with whom you are working. Ask if they will help you by discussing their children.

   2. Take a tape recorder and record your conversation so that you can analyse the information after the interview. Spend some time explaining what you are doing and make sure that they are relaxed. Then ask them to describe the behaviour/personality of their child as fully as possible. Do not interrupt, unless you need to clarify what they have said. When they have finished make sure they do not want to add anything else. Before leaving arrange to see them again to discuss your findings.

   3. Transcribe the tape recording of the Child Characterization Sketch only. If any parts are unintelligible or unclear simply put a dash to represent this.

   4. Analyse the transcribed text using the rules listed above.

   5. Consider the results carefully. Put yourself in the parent's shoes and try to see if you can see the child as she/he does. What conclusions can you draw? For example, has the parent focused upon certain areas of child behaviour and ignored others? Can you predict how the parent would behave in various situations? Make a note of your conclusions.

   6. Meet the parent again and discuss your findings. Ask the parent to evaluate your conclusions and predictions.

CHAPTER 4

Understanding Parents

'Why do we have children?' 'What is good parenting?' Questions like these are discussed frequently. They appear deceptively simple, for there are no well formulated and generally accepted models from which to provide definite answers. Yet a central aim of working with parents is to foster and strengthen so-called parenting skills in order to benefit the child's development.

To do this, professionals require a set of frameworks to help them make sense of parenting, families and reactions to handicap. They need some knowledge of the major characteristics of parenting and families in relation to the well-being and development of the child. They need some conception of what parents value in being parents and a framework to understand the likely reactions of parents to having a child with special needs. They need knowledge of the ways in which family members influence each other and how families function. Most importantly, if they are going to offer practical assistance, they need a framework to determine how to help families to take action to prevent or reduce a problem. We would emphasize again, however, that although there is much written about parents of children with special needs (e.g. Marion, 1981; Abidin, 1980; Berger, 1981; Paul, 1981; Hannam, 1980; Miezio, 1983), there is little unequivocal knowledge in many of these areas, and so the frameworks discussed are necessarily general and cannot be imposed on individual parents or families. We will consider the frameworks for understanding parents, their functions and their adjustment to a child with special needs in this chapter, and the family as a whole and its wider social network in the next.

We will begin with an example. Look at the picture in Figure

44

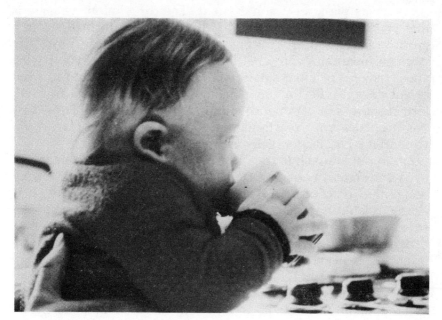

Figure 4

4. If we tell you that this baby is quite ordinary with no known problems and ask you how old you think he is, what will you answer? How confident are you in your answer? What gives you this confidence? Presumably it depends on your knowledge and experience of young children accumulated over many years from both formal and informal sources. Much of this type of 'normative' knowledge is derived from the common pool of information and values in our culture which we acquire during our life from everyday events and from formal education. You probably know that 'normal' babies can grasp and drink from a cup around 5 to 9 months of age, and so you should feel relatively confident in answering 5 to 9 months to the question.

Now, what if we tell you this child has Zenkov–Sotti syndrome. It is a chromosomal abnormality associated with severe intellectual impairment and developmental delay; there are abnormalities in skeletal growth and structure, muscle tone, flexion of joints and coordination, and there is an increased risk of cardiac, respiratory, visual and auditory disorders and higher rates of mortality. Now, how old do you think the baby is? Are you as certain? Most people guess at any age between one and three years and have considerable uncertainty.

In fact, the baby has Down's Syndrome. Zenkov–Sotti syndrome is, as far as we know, non-existent. The description we gave is that of Down's Syndrome and is the kind of information often given to parents. Can you guess how old the child is now? Are you still uncertain? On what body of knowledge are you basing your answer? To what extent is it factually accurate and to what extent does it reflect a generalized stereotype, acquired from informal sources or experience with individual children? How does this influence your reactions and feelings? How anxious would you feel if your answer really mattered?

Try to put yourself in the place of his parents at this time. Since he is your child, your uncertainty and associated anxiety cannot be ignored or considered in a detached or objective way. It is closely related to your feelings for him and your need to understand and help him. If you lack a construct system from which to decide if he is developing reasonably well or to anticipate future progress, you are likely to experience increased anxiety. Since many handicapping conditions are not remediable, this uncertainty is a life-long issue. This uncertainty may also affect how you feel about your ability to help and decide what is best. You may question your competence and act with less confidence.

Clearly, the emotional relationship between parent and child and the associated feelings and reactions are central to parenting. As noted in Chapter 2, the strong attachment that most parents have to the child differentiates them from the professional. It can result in strong partiality, with parent or family members being more likely to act in altruistic and unselfish ways. The child can make demands which, except in the context of such a relationship, would be seen as unreasonable. He/she also evokes a range of strong feelings and a range of hopes and aspirations. What are these feelings or reactions? What do we understand by emotion? Since this is central to parenting and handicap, we will briefly discuss it in terms of Personal Construct Theory. McCoy (1977) provides a more extensive exploration and elaboration.

Understanding Emotion

A particularly useful aspect of Personal Construct Theory is the way in which emotion is understood. It is unusual in the sense that the dichotomy traditionally made between feelings/emotions and thinking is not accepted as valuable. Instead, emotions are defined in relation to the processes of construing. Emotions are not, therefore, defined by physiological arousal, nor are they vague, nebulous concepts, assuming varying degrees of irrationality, and therefore being potentially abnormal and alien. Concepts such as anxiety, threat and guilt are understood as the individual's awareness of change or imminent change in aspects of his/her construct system. They refer to the individuals' own constructions about the ways they are currently understanding events, and they are essentially related to the process of change in that understanding. They are not therefore seen as 'things' to be treated, stopped or prevented, but as functional in the process of reconstruction.

Reconstruction or change is viewed in terms of invalidation of existing constructs and a process called the CPC cycle. This refers to the stages of reconstruction in which alternative ways of viewing events are considered (Circumspection), particular ways of understanding are adopted and others rejected (Pre-emption), and events become sufficiently meaningful for a course of action to be plotted (Control).

Hence, anxiety is defined as the awareness that the events with which one is confronted lie mostly outside the range of convenience of one's construct system. Range of convenience refers to the assumption that any construct or construct system applies only to some events and not to others. The implication of this definition of anxiety is that the individual cannot, and is aware that he/she cannot, make sense of an event or situation and will, therefore, experience uncertainty. This results in the person being more likely to try to change the way he/she construes the world in order to make sense of the new experience and to reduce this anxiety/uncertainty.

Guilt is defined as the awareness of dislodgement of the self from one's core role structure. The core role structure refers to central aspects of the construct system to do with the way the individual makes sense of his/her own behaviour. It relates to what otherwise may be called the self-concept, self-image or self-identity. This definition of guilt, therefore, expresses the situation of people aware of themselves as not acting in ways that they would have expected themselves to act. Again, therefore, guilt is resolved when people reconstrue themselves and their own behaviour.

Threat is defined as the awareness of imminent comprehensive change in one's core structures. This means that the person's major beliefs about the world, or part of it, are being invalidated, and as a consequence events become incomprehensible and chaotic.

In Personal Construct Theory, therefore, there are 'feelings' in the sense that the individual is aware of something, or is making a discrimination between events. The events in this case, however, are not external but are the person's own constructs. Feeling may refer to the awareness of the processes of construing, as emotion is defined, but in general means the same as to construe. For example, to feel resentment means to construe an external event as 'unfair' as opposed to 'fair'. To feel rejected is to construe another as 'pushing you away' as opposed to 'valuing you'. Any behaviour that is shown as a result of such feelings or emotions is not the emotion *per se*, but is a reaction to it. It is, therefore, worth making a distinction between emotion and reaction. Reactions, however caused, are usually the immediate, observed behaviour in a situation and not necessarily understandable. One parent may react angrily to the news that their child has a handicap or requires special help; another may cry or become 'numb'. Some may deny the situation or avoid any information which confirms or confronts them with the reality of the diagnosis. All may be construed as experiencing invalidation of their existing constructs about the child and themselves. Their reactions can be seen as ways of gaining the necessary information and time to reconstruct a different understanding.

A final, and most pertinent example, is the construct of attachment. Whilst most people have an awareness of attachment, definitions are elusive and often restricted to reactions or associated behaviours. In the literature on infant development, for example, it is inferred from the infants' reactions to separations and reunions with the primary caretaker and from reactions to strangers. It is also predominantly concerned with infants' attachments to adults and not adult to child attachment. The latter is inferred from the emotional reactions of the adult to the behaviour of the child, in expressing verbally or behaviourally what can be inferred as joy, pride or anger. Thus, the opposite of attachment is not rejection or anger, but indifference.

Attachment is also an important explanatory concept for bereavement. Bereavement is seen as the loss of the attachment object, either a person or thing. Loss implies that something needed for one's wellbeing is missing. McCoy argues that attachment or love, in terms of Personal Construct Theory, can be defined as 'the awareness of the validation of one's core structure'. In other words, one is completed by the other person and it is the awareness of this that is the foundation of the relationship. The other person validates one's beliefs about oneself and their actions support and validate the core role structure or one's self-identity. Loss, therefore, removes a source of validation and awareness of completeness and certainty. Since the core structure is under constant review or change, the greater the need for this validation, the greater the awareness of loss. Similarly, if the core structure is seen as a changing construct, then attachment is not constant.

The birth of a child with a handicap and the recognition that the child is not what one wanted or expected, may invalidate the core structures. Considerable reconstruction is therefore required and will, as discussed later, require a construction of the child as a person and separate from the handicap. It is difficult to see how anyone can be attached to a handicap, and therefore parents and professionals must develop a construct system which goes beyond the impairment to the person and which gives that person value. As the child grows and changes and the needs and sources of validation change, so the nature of attachment may change.

Parenting

The main factors which relate to parenting and which affect the child's well-being are:

(i)   the quality of the physical environment;
(ii)   the expression of warmth and affection toward the child;
(iii)   sensitivity to the child's needs as reflected in the quality of interactions;
(iv)   the use of control over the child's actions;
(v)   active involvement with the child.

(i)   *The Quality of the Physical Environment*

Apart from good physical care, the opportunities provided by the physical environment to explore and learn in a variety of settings is important. Studies of both ordinary children and those with special needs report high correlations between availability of books, toys and child-oriented activities in the home and measures of the child's development. Not only is this seen in the actual materials available but in the range of new and varied experiences presented. Different situations and settings can be seen as challenging the child's construct system and offering new perspectives. If parents cannot provide this variety because of restricted time and finances, or fail to recognize its importance, then the child's development may be inhibited.

The recognition of these factors has influenced the spread of play-groups, nursery schools and the broadening of the school curriculum. The objectives are less tangible than in specific teaching sessions, and it is certainly less easy to demonstrate change. Consequently, such provision is associated with more uncertainty or may often be overlooked or taken for granted. Sharing with parents the justification and evidence that it is important can reinforce their feelings of competence in that they are providing positive experiences for their child. This has to include, however, guidance on the appropriateness of such experiences in relation to the child's abilities and developmental level. Without such justification, much of the advice or supportive statements given, become mere platitudes which do little to reduce uncertainty or reinforce confidence.

(ii) Warmth and Affection

A basic need for all children is to feel loved, cared for, valued and respected, in order for them to develop a positive self-image, and to value and respect themselves. Our constructions of what we are like and how competent we are, arise not just from our ability to act on and develop control and mastery over the environment, but also from how others act towards us and how we construe these actions in terms of their perceptions of us. Thus, as argued earlier, mutual attachment or love between parent and child are a foundation for wellbeing and validation of one's self constructions. Such constructs develop early in life and, for most children, in the context of the family and the immediate home environment. If they feel secure and have a stable emotional base, they can explore outward into the wider physical and social world. Of course, love and valuing another are not identical. The latter depends much upon the constructs one has about the characteristics of others. Value relates to construing that the other person has positive characteristics. In the case of the child with special needs, parents and professionals frequently need to reappraise their value system in general and in relation to the child. For example, a positive self-image is hardly likely to be fostered if the child is treated as a mere recipient of family help. A positive appreciation of how the child contributes to the family is needed in order to develop ways for the child to participate actively in the family.

(iii) Sensitivity to the Child's Needs

To develop a positive self-image in the child, parents must be sensitive to the child's needs which will be seen in the quality of interaction with the child. This involves providing opportunities for the child to act and express him/herself, with parents then reacting positively and elaborating upon these actions, in order to encourage the child's validation and development of constructs. Studies of non-handicapped and handicapped infants are increasingly finding that the nature of parent–child interactions in the early months (and presumably this is a continual process) correlate with later cognitive and emotional development (Gottfried, 1984). There is also evidence that the interaction between parents and their handicapped child may be qualitatively different from parents and their non-handicapped children. It is suggested that this is due to differences in the child's social and communicative skills and in the case of mental handicap a slower ability to process information and react to it. It also relates to the parents' constructions of the child and of how he/she responds in a given situation. Thus, if a baby does not respond with a smile within the normally expected time, the mother may interpret this as an inability to respond and either increase her attempts to gain a response or stop trying, instead of exploring different rates and styles of interaction. The analogy can be extended to teachers where there is much evidence demonstrating the effect of expectations (the teachers' construct system of the child) and how this influences their interactions with the child.

For this reason, it is important that both parents and professionals review their ideas about the child fairly regularly and consider how this influences their daily interactions. As noted in Chapter 2, parental interactions are more likely to be spontaneous and opportunistic than those of a professional, but this does not imply they should be random or inconsistent. Regularity and consistency are important for learning; it reduces uncertainty. The art is in providing sufficient variety to challenge current constructs and encourage adaptation and generalization, yet sufficient consistency and regularity to form a secure and familiar base from which to explore. If the child is going to develop self-regulation or autonomy, interactions within this variety of settings have to be under his/her control to varying degrees. Thus, an interactive style which is mainly impositional and highly didactic is unlikely to facilitate this.

This issue is highlighted in the methods used to control the child's behaviour in the context of social and moral rules.

(iv) Control

Positive development is often found to be associated with relative consistency in demands and in the use of censure, and a consistency in the standards and models of behaviour presented to the child. It is generally accepted that regulating behaviour through reasoning with the child is the appropriate method. The aim is to develop constructs which allow the child to anticipate the expectations of others in social interactions and the consequences of various actions. This reduces uncertainty and increases confidence in establishing relationships. This, of course, demands some ability on the part of the child to reason or learn from the social models presented and therefore is related to maturity and developmental level.

This area is often a source of conflict between parents and professionals. Frequently it concerns value judgements of what is acceptable and appropriate behaviour. Often it reflects the difference between parent and professional roles, and/or cultural differences. The strong emotional relationship between parent and child will often interact with feelings such as protectiveness or resentment, which the professional is unlikely to share. Equally, the child's constructs of the parent and professional will influence their acceptance or reactions to censure. This is seen in the child's rate of compliance, which appears to be lower in parent–child than teacher–child interactions. Indeed, it may be that it is only in the relative safety of a positive emotional relationship that the child can first explore the rules of social interaction and his/her developing independence. Thus, he/she is more likely to test these out with parents than with others. These limits are shown in the consistent presentation of models and standards of expected behaviours. Where this consistency is lacking and/or where the emotional base is uncertain, then the child is likely to experience anxiety and develop behaviour difficulties.

The lower compliance rate to parental demands may be seen by professionals as too inconsistent. However, the freedom or amount of control the parent gives the child may be necessary and more appropriate for the child to explore the rules, because of their special relationship. Ideally, therefore, parents and professionals must, whilst recognizing their differences and the child's constructs of them, develop and share a mutually agreed framework to regulate their interactions with the child.

(v) Active Involvement

The active involvement of parents with their children in such activities as play, talking and reading is strongly associated with developmental outcomes. Again, it is not just a case of quantity but the qualitative nature of the interaction. Presumably, if parents give priority to such activities, then they construe them as important in terms of influencing the child's development. In spending time with the child, parents are also indicating that they value the child and enjoy his/her company. Whilst the majority of interactions with the child are spontaneous and not structured intentional acts, most parents do try to teach their children some things at some times. They relate their attempts to their view of the child's current ability as shown in such commonly heard phrases as, 'It's about time you learnt to do that for yourself' or 'At your age you should be able to do that'. This may often be followed by some teaching approach using modelling, prompting, verbal exposition, etc.

For most parents the decision to carry out the teaching is an opportunistic reaction to a current event. Few establish an objective or a well-formulated curriculum through which they systematically work. Therefore, in fostering active parental involvement with the child, the professional will need to delineate the current level of involvement and the 'natural' style of teaching used by parents. They should then try to build on this rather than impose a style that may be contrived. The style and the areas focused on by the parent will depend upon how worthwhile they construe the knowledge or skill to be for the child and their constructions of the child's and their own abilities. It is these aspects which are likely to be highly influenced by the recognition of a handicap in the child and, therefore, require careful appraisal by the professional.

The importance of the parents' constructs of child rearing, development and education is clearly reflected in the frequent research findings of a strong relationship between parental beliefs and measures of child development. One enduring aspect of Head-start type programmes (see Chapter 7) for disadvantaged families appears to be positive changes in parental attitude and aspirations for the child and also changes in the child's attitude to school and him/herself. Numerous studies have also reported a strong relationship between parental education, social class and children's development and scholastic attainments. Whilst the relationship between parental education and child development is often discussed in terms of genetic endowment, the level of parental education is also related to socio-economic factors, values and aspirations. More educated parents may be more able and willing to ensure educational opportunities for the child which, in the case of organically handicapped children, may counteract the dangers of secondary handicap. Studies have reported that some neurological abnormalities noted in the first year of life were

only associated with poor outcomes in later years for socially disadvantaged children. The interaction between parent and child
variables is also indicated in studies of emotional difficulties,
where prognosis is highly associated with parental competence
in interaction skills.

Finally, one cannot, of course, directly generalize from these
broad findings to individual cases. Most people will be aware of
children who are apparently undamaged and prosper despite
what appear to be adverse and unsupporting environmental conditions and parenting. Clearly parenting is a complex interaction
of many variables and, as stated earlier, there is a current lack
of knowledge about the extent and relative importance of such
variables.

Feelings, Reactions and Disability

Whether a parent or professional, one's feelings and reactions
to a child's disability strongly influence the relationship established with the child. As discussed earlier, emotions such as threat,
guilt and anxiety can be construed positively in relation to their
role in the process of change in the construct system. Since they
are defined in terms of an awareness of change, they can be viewed
as essential components of the process of change, and as signals
for the need to change. The importance of this viewpoint can
be illustrated in the context of giving the news to parents that
their child or baby has a handicap. Many studies report a high
rate of parental dissatisfaction about how this was done. Frequently noted, for example, is the witholding of the news by professionals or denying the parents' concerns; unsympathetic ways
of giving the information; lack of privacy and/or time to take in
the information.

Often, professionals appear to interpret parental anger or dissatisfaction as an inevitable consequence of their feelings of 'guilt'
or 'unfairness'. This can be seen as applying a pathological framework to explain parental dissatisfaction and it does little to facilitate
ways of positively helping. Alternatively, one could construe the
parents as feeling that a stigma is attached to having a child with
a handicap, and/or that they will question their competence in
coping with the child's condition. Thus, witholding information
and giving explanations that are not understood could inadvertently confirm their feelings. Their reactions, therefore, relate to
their awareness that their construct system is not able to make
sense of the new information and that what is being done to them

is frustrating or ignoring this need. Hence, a policy which takes this into account and which demonstrates that they and the child are valued and respected is required. Telling parents in a sharp or hasty way, in a public place, with no opportunity to ask questions does not convey respect; quite the reverse.

Reactions of anger and dissatisfaction have been found to be considerably less where parents are told (i) as soon as possible, (ii) together, (iii) sympathetically, but with a balanced honest appraisal of implications which do not just list negative aspects, (iv) in a private place with time to react, (v) in a series of planned discussions of practical and relevant information, and (vi) that there will be continuity of service support. In the case of infants in hospital, having the baby present, with the professional showing, by playing with the child, that he/she is not rejected or ignored, as 'not worthy of attention', is also helpful. Such parents also seem to adjust more quickly and establish more positive relationships with each other, the child and the professionals. This suggests that they have been assisted in making necessary changes in their construct system. Although little is known about the situation where parents are told of apparently less severe problems, nevertheless, it must be realized that it is ultimately the constructs of the parents, not the professional, that determine the severity of the reaction. Telling parents with high academic aspirations that their child is slightly delayed in reading or expressive language development may be very traumatic and many teachers and therapists have experienced surprise at the degree of parental denial or questioning of the conclusions.

For severe events, like the birth of a disabled child or bereavement, a number of stage models of feelings and reactions have been suggested. The stages are meant to highlight the predominant reactions in the process of adaptation to such news, and all models emphasize that no person moves through the stages discretely or sequentially. Commonly people oscillate between stages and there are often reversals. Even so, the models do appear to provide useful frameworks to guide professionals in these situations (Blaches, 1984).

To illustrate one such model briefly, the first phase is one of *shock*. Parents often describe a numbness and paralysis of action, whilst being psychologically disorganized, irrational and confused. This can last for minutes or days. They require support and sympathetic understanding. This stage can be seen as involving massive anxiety (i.e. inability to construe), threat (i.e. invalidation of previous constructs) or possibly guilt (seeing oneself in a completely new light) and therefore it may be associated with very low self-confidence, which McCoy (1977) defines as the awareness of the goodness of fit of the self in one's core role structure. The event challenges the whole of the parents' construct system for making sense of events generally, as well as for making sense of him/herself in relation to these events (the core role structure).

The second phase, though related to shock, has been called the *reaction phase*. Parents express reactions such as anger, denial, resentment, disbelief, and feelings such as sorrow, loss, anxiety, guilt, protectiveness. This is the beginning of the CPC cycle (Circumspective, Pre-emption and Control Cycle). Rather than interpreting such reactions as irrational, abnormal or pathological, this idea leads one to construe them as evidence of actually exploring the situation (i.e. circumspection). As noted in Chapter 3, it is the beginning of the process of reconstruction, with reactions and statements, being seen not as pathology, but as strategies to test ideas and to reconstrue. Denying the diagnosis, for example, provides a temporary solution to the inability to understand what is happening. This in itself is an exploration, a test of one set of ideas, because by using constructs that were available before the diagnosis allows them to be validated or otherwise in the new situation. Anger directed either at professionals or inwardly at the parent him/herself, again allows exploration of causal aspects of the situation. Questioning the diagnosis generally, even asking for a second opinion, should not be interpreted as an attack on the professional, nor as unwillingness to accept, but as an obvious step in reconstructing and understanding what has occurred. Since some parents may sensibly construe experts as fallible, it is not unreasonable to test this by demanding independent evidence before embarking upon major reconstruction.

To aid this process the parents require careful and well organized counselling as elaborated in Chapter 6. Considerable reconstruction is needed and whilst the reactions may soon alter, the underlying emotions may endure for long periods and some may never be resolved. Chronic sorrow or resentment of the handicap, is often reported by parents. Even so most do begin to change and a new phase termed the *adaptation phase* becomes predominant. It is signalled when parents begin to ask such questions as, 'What can be done?' which implies a new set of needs. In Personal Construct Theory terms it is seen as pre-emption in that the parent has adopted at least a nucleus of constructs that enable him/her to make sense of him/herself and the situation and to appraise possible courses of action. They require, therefore, accurate information about possible help and support. Soon they ask

'How can we help?' which signals that they are moving into the *orientation phase* when they begin to organize, seek help, establish new routines, plan resources and learn new skills. In the CPC Cycle, this is the stage of control, where parents have reconstrued sufficiently to 'know' what to do and begin to act on the problems confronting them. To do so, they require a regular support which offers practical advice and goal setting which takes into account the family needs. Central to the process of adaptation is the understanding of parental emotions. Classifications of parent feelings and reactions have been attempted and their implications explored (MacKeith, 1973).

The literature of this area mainly covers parental reactions expressed overtly in words or acts, or feelings which are really the interpretations or constructions that the parents are placing upon events outside and inside themselves. What is most important is that such feelings, whatever their content, are not without purpose. Though perhaps not consciously so, they are a major part of the process of change in the construct system and are intimately related to reconstruing events in a different way. Feelings will actually be the themes and content of the parents' emerging construct systems. They are the constructs that parents are adopting, even temporarily, as hypotheses to be tested. In all, therefore, they are exploratory strategies contributing to the eventual understanding of the situation confronting the parents and their eventual level of adaptation. For example, what some authors have called parental guilt can be reinterpreted as the parents construing themselves as 'the cause of the problem' or construing themselves as 'being to blame'. Only by construing in this way, are they able to consider the validity or otherwise of this way of viewing the situation. By avoiding this construction, they would be unable to test the hypothesis. By thinking of each topic to be discussed below as hypotheses or constructs being tested/explored, a framework should be provided to give coherence to what can be seen as a list of discrete unrelated adjectives, which in the past have been viewed as frequently found, but of little value in indicating helpful action.

Since professionals also have feelings and reactions to handicap, they too must consider what these are and how they affect their actions. Recognizing shared reactions and feelings can create a basis for empathy, or if opposed, likely areas of conflict. Often people are surprised or shocked at the range and strength of their reactions and feelings and what they indicate about their self-concept or core role structures.

Protectiveness

Most people have some feelings of protectiveness towards an infant, a child who is ill or one with a visible handicap. These feelings usually lead the parent toward developing a loving and caring relationship with the child. However, such feelings can become extreme. Parents may become particularly sensitive to any implied suggestion of criticism or negative reaction toward the child. This can interact with their own feelings of negativism, resentment and anger, which may then be reflected in a negative reaction toward the perceived critic. An excessively strong protective reaction can also cause an imbalance within the family, particularly in relation to other children. It may even become a set pattern in which the development of the child's independence is prevented by not being allowed to take reasonable risks in exploring the environment. Such parents need to explore the possible consequences of their protectiveness, as opposed to being accused of overprotection.

Revulsion

Revulsion may be too strong a word, but it does focus attention on a set of constructs which are not uncommon. However, expressing such constructs is rare because of the unwarranted implication that it reflects an uncaring person. Many people can have deep feelings of 'revulsion' about a disability, even old age, yet be caring. It is helpful to recognize these and then begin to explore their meaning, since they will influence actions towards the disabled person. Not looking at someone during interaction certainly conveys a strong message that is easily interpreted as revulsion. One can also be 'revolted' by particular attributes of a person, such as disfigurement, constant dribbling or incontinence. Some children who have a physical handicap are well integrated whilst others with a severe skin disorder are not.

Such feelings are often closely associated with anxiety; we tend to fear that which we do not understand or that which arouses threat. One reaction to anxiety is the avoidance of what is perceived as the source of the anxiety, the disabled person, and this may be seen in lack of involvement or rejection.

Rejection

Rejection is another strong and all too frequently used word with many connotations. It is a reaction; it does not indicate why the person is avoiding the situation. Again, it is necessary to explore underlying constructs in order to gain an understanding of the reaction. Thus parents who initially appear to 'reject' the child are often indicating they need time and information to be able to reconstrue, and it is unhelpful to label them as uncaring, as is suggested by using the term rejection. Rejection is not the opposite of attachment, which we have argued is indifference.

Resentment

Though associated with rejection and revulsion, resentment is not quite the same. One can resent the handicap on behalf of the child, and/or resent the child. The former can have positive outcomes such as the determination to act on the child's behalf and to help. In the case of the latter one may find lack of involvement and care or hostility. Resentment can also be felt in relation to the restrictions that the demands made by the child's handicap has on individual or family functions, or when conflict arises between family members concerning the child.

Most parents will experience feelings of protectiveness and revulsion or resentment, and it is not uncommon for parents to say that they love the child but resent the handicap. The attempt to balance and reconcile the two may produce conflict within individuals and between family members. A recognition that such feelings are not abnormal and that the anxiety felt is a healthy indication of change can help.

Professionals will also be influenced by these feelings. Most caring professionals will tend toward feelings of protectiveness given that they have usually selected to work in the field of special needs. They will also have a more developed framework to understand the child's condition or special needs. Thus, they may find it difficult to understand and interact with parents who appear uncaring or rejecting, particularly in the first meetings. Since many parents assume the professional is judging their reactions, and what type of parents they are, a situation is produced for potential conflict. Professionals need, therefore, to avoid taking sides and to avoid any indication that they disapprove of the parent's behaviour.

Reproductive Inadequacy

To reproduce means to produce a copy and there appears to be a fundamental desire in most human beings to have children and

possibly to see them as extensions of themselves. In cases of handicap, it is suggested that parents may have feelings of reproductive
inadequacy. In some cases, the sexual relationship of partners
can be affected, apparently because of the possibility of having
another handicapped child. Information on reproductive risk and
cause are of great importance at this time. Parents, particularly
when the handicapped child is their first, often recognize these
feelings later after the birth of a non-handicapped child:

> It wasn't until he was born and we knew he was O.K. that I realised
> how much it meant to me to produce a normal baby.

As discussed earlier in the chapter, the loved or attached person
(in this case the child) validates one's beliefs about oneself (one's
core role structure). Thus the strong desire to have children may
be seen as enabling such validation in that it may endorse one's
competence as a person. It may also enhance one's self-image
more generally, since the child's characteristics may be seen as
reflecting on the parents.

However, the recognition that the child is handicapped, or less
than one expected, invalidates the core role structure and produces
uncertainty and anxiety. Attachment, in terms of the other person
completing or validating oneself is difficult. A sense of loss, uncertainty and anxiety about one's competence are therefore likely.
Striking deep at the core role structure, which has developed over
many years, these reactions are painful or difficult to resolve.
Other family members will also be affected. Siblings can experience
feelings of family or self inadequacy in reproduction and one can
find parents and grandparents reproaching each other:

> We have not had anything like this on our side of the family.

Such feelings are likely to endure and can surface later, at the
time of the birth of a non-handicapped baby to a relative or friend,
or when siblings are teased or questioned about their brother or
sister. Again, they have to be recognized and discussed so that
understanding will reduce the anxieties felt.

Self Competence

Similarly, feelings about one's competence to provide and care
for a child are common whether handicapped or not. Earlier self-
confidence was defined (McCoy, 1977) as the awareness of the
goodness of fit of oneself into the core role structure. It is the
extent to which one construes oneself as capable of being what

one believes. Thus the inability to construe the handicap, what can be done or future implications is likely to create an imbalance between what one has believed about oneself in the past and what will be necessary in the future. Such feelings can make parents particularly sensitive to innuendo or suggestions that they cannot cope.

Many parents will also be grateful to professionals who demonstrate appropriate knowledge and competence and therefore pressurize them (both overtly and covertly) into situations which encourage dependency. In these circumstances the professional can easily slip into the pattern of telling parents what to do and when to do it; of protecting them from the demands and responsibility of decision making; of offering apparent solutions too quickly without joint discussion (i.e. slipping into the expert model).

Although this may be a useful short-term strategy on the part of the professional, the long term implications are costly, because it is likely that dependency may either slow down the process of the parents rebuilding their own construct system or impose upon them a model that is not appropriate to them as individuals. In the former case the parents will be inadequately prepared to cope with future events and, in the latter, may be confronted with extra stresses arising from the conflicts emerging from how they actually construe themselves and how they feel they should be. Thus whilst professionals may take great satisfaction (find validation for their own core role structure) when parents say: 'We couldn't manage without you', this must surely be a sign that the professional has much more work to do and that a change in strategy is required.

Both parents and professionals will have feelings of inadequacy which may be expressed in defensive reactions to criticism. If the parent questions professional advice, for example, by asking for a second opinion or by commenting critically on what was done, professionals may, because of their sense of inadequacy, react defensively. Such reactions may reduce parental confidence in services and are likely to damage the relationship. Similarly, when parents receive conflicting advice from professional sources or even more so, criticism of one source by another, this must increase their uncertainty and shake their confidence. Often contradiction is related to lack of current knowledge and the fact that such children vary so much, one cannot generalize but must work through individual needs and resources. In such cases this has to be admitted and discussed; sharing these uncertainties can be a positive strategy. But sometimes it clearly relates to our feelings of inadequacy. By denigrating others one feels one's own self-esteem is raised. It does not, however, facilitate the establishment of mutual respect and confidence.

Embarrassment and Guilt

Embarrassment can be defined as the awareness that you are not what you believe another has construed you to be. The parents who feel this may, therefore, avoid social contacts and may feel that they have failed. To prevent such a situation, it is important for friends, neighbours and professionals to accept them and not to suggest otherwise inadvertently. Friends and neighbours who avoid the parents of a handicapped child because they do not know how to deal with the mother, are expressing their own anxiety, but may be construed by the parents as commenting negatively upon them. A similar interpretation may occur if the doctor or teacher is curt or circumlocutory, avoids eye contact and fidgets when telling the parent about the results of their assessment.

Uncertainty or anxiety in the parents may encourage this misinterpretation of cues given by others. Reactions to this, other than avoiding social contact, are to become defiant, aggressive and hostile, or to act apologetically. In the former case the parent may be extorting validational evidence of their own view of events by overruling the views of others (whatever they may be). In the latter, they are adopting, rightly or wrongly, the perceived framework of others, that there is a stigma associated with their situation. Such a reaction may be seen in the constant tendency to explain the child's behaviour to other people, including strangers.

These reactions can be prevented by professionals not acting in ways that can be misconstrued by the parents as negative. Alternatively, such issues can be openly addressed in counselling with the parents. Sensitive discussion may enable parents to broach the subject of the handicap with others in ways that allow open communication and minimize misconstruction.

The notion of embarrassment as defined here differs from the definition of guilt discussed earlier in the chapter, in that guilt is the awareness of a discrepancy between one's behaviour and one's own expectations of oneself. Embarrassment is defined in relation to the expectations of others. Such a distinction perhaps helps to clarify the overemphasis that has been given in the past to guilt as a parental reaction.

Nevertheless, despite this overemphasis, parents may realistically experience guilt when their actions have been in some way responsible for the child's special needs. This may vary from the situation of vaccine damage to where they have actively injured the child or done so by carelessness. This emotion may also arise from sources such as (i) not doing enough to help the child subsequently; (ii) not knowing enough about what to do; or (iii) not doing enough for the rest of the family, because of the needs of the special child. Again, the importance of open discussion is indicated in that parents may need to be helped to reconstrue their causal role in the creation of the problem and the extent to which they can expect to be instrumental in the solution.

Concluding Comments

We have attempted to give a framework in which to consider the role of parents and their reactions to having a child with special needs. We have tried to simplify what is undoubtedly a most complex area, yet at the same time to illustrate the complexity and the individuality of parental reactions. With reference to Personal Construct Theory a more positive and functional orientation is given to parental feelings and reactions, which are often regarded as pathological, particularly when what they show does not make sense to the professional. Of course parents do not exist in isolation. They influence and are influenced in turn by their interactions with their other children, their own parents and others in their extended family and by their friends and neighbours. Since these influences are important, we shall provide relevant frameworks to help make sense of them in the next chapter.

Practical Exercise

A major difficulty that parents have to resolve, and professionals may fail to consider, is the separation of the ways they construe the child from the ways in which they construe the child's impairment, handicap or special need. It may be, for example, that resentment of the handicap is manifested as resentment of the child. By failing to separate the two, parents may feel that they are, for example, uncaring or rejecting, and therefore may feel guilt in the sense of construing themselves in ways that they see as uncharacteristic. Such experiences can only add unnecessarily to their difficulties. Although this situation is not easily clarified, the following exercise may be useful:

1. Seek the co-operation of a parent with a child with special needs. Carefully explain that you are involved in a learning exercise and describe openly and accurately what you would like to do.

2. Elicit the ways the parent has of construing his/her child by using the Child Characterization Sketch described in Chapter 3.
3. Record the description of the child either on a cassette recorder or by taking comprehensive notes as the parent talks.
4. Go slowly through the recording or notes and make a list in co-operation and discussion with the parent of his/her major constructs.
5. Once you have a list, ask the parent to consider each construct in turn and to state what he/she would consider to be the opposite of each characteristic. Note this down beside each construct in the list.
6. This means that you should have a list of bipolar constructs that look something like the following:

    | He loves to entertain others | Shy. |
    | Loving | Indifferent. |
    | Can get bad tempered | Always placid. |
    | Very distractible | Concentrates well |
    | etc. . . . | |

7. Aim to make a list of 10 to 20 constructs at most, though of course this is dependent upon how much or how little the parent had to say about the child.
8. Take the first construct and ask the parent to think of the two poles as a dimension on which the child's position could be plotted. Suggest a 5-point scale with '5' indicating close agreement with the pole on the left, '1' indicating close agreement with the other pole, and points '2', '3' and '4' being intermediate.
9. Ask the parent to decide how he/she would rate the child on the first construct, and note the figure by the side.
10. Now repeat this in turn for each of the following constructs, so that the child is given a score on all the dimensions.
11. These scores, written down beside their appropriate constructs will give a simple profile of how the parent construes the child on the set of constructs.
12. It is now possible to determine the extent to which the parent's constructions of the child and his/her constructions of the child's problem/difficulties are linked by asking the parent to imagine what would happen to the child on each of the listed constructs if the impairment/problem no longer existed.
13. The way of doing this is to take each construct in turn and to ask the parent whether the child would change

on the construct, if his/her difficulties were to disappear.
14. You now have a number of 'Yes' and 'No' answers about whether the constructs would change or not. The more 'No' decisions, the more likely the parent is to be totally separating the way he/she construes the child from his/her problem. The more 'Yes' decisions, the more the constructions of the child are intimately related to the impairment. An example is shown in Figure 5. This mother in general

CONSTRUCTS		RATING*	CHANGE
A	B		
Well behaved	Naughty	5	YES
Active	Passive	3	YES
Quiet	Noisey	4	YES
Loving	Not loving	5	YES
Inquisitive	Uninquisitive	1	YES
Irritable	Placid	2	YES
Obedient	Disobedient	5	YES
Happy	Sad	5	NO
Intelligent	Not intelligent	2	YES
Easily managed	Difficult	5	YES
Dependent	Independent	5	YES
Friendly	Unfriendly	5	YES
Easily distracted	Not distractable	3	YES
Patient	Impatient	5	YES

*5 refers to complete agreement with column A, and 1 to complete agreement with column B.

Figure 5 Example Profile: A mother's ratings (5 point scale) on a set of constructs and her judgements about whether the rating would change if the child were no longer intellectually impaired.

views her child very positively, but construes almost all the constructs as related to the child's severe intellectual impairment.
15. Whatever the specific results, it is valuable to discuss them fully with the parents in order to investigate their interpretation of them.

CHAPTER 5

Understanding Families
in the Community

> Everyone who came kept asking questions about the baby – telling
> me what could be done for him; what was wrong – but nobody
> asked how I felt, what I needed. I had to ask about how it would
> change us as a family.

Services in the field of children with special needs understandably
have a strong child focus. Paediatricians, teachers, speech therapists, occupational therapists and specialized health visitors or
social workers are highly trained to have specific expertise in a
relatively well-defined area to do with the child. The inherent
danger is that they may overlook the needs of other family
members or fail to recognize the important influences the family
has on the child's development and welfare. Alternatively, just
as they may concentrate on one aspect of the child and neglect
the whole child, they may seek out and concentrate on one aspect
of the family. They may, for example, fail to consider the implications of their advice on other members of the family and the
balance of needs and resources operating within the family.

This is becoming more important for families with a severely
handicapped member as society moves towards the reality of community care. Care in the community, as opposed to specialized
residential facilities, largely means care by families with support
from a network made up of extended family members, friends
and neighbours, as well as professionals and services (i.e. the
informal and formal network). Increasingly, clinical and research
findings are indicating the importance of the informal network
in helping families to care for children with special needs at home
and in the community. Indeed there is evidence that the informal
network is, in many instances, far more influential than the formal
support given.

This has widespread implications for professionals, both at the planning and organizational level and at the face-to-face level, in terms of skills and conceptual frameworks. For example, as we will discuss throughout this chapter, professionals should not construe themselves as the major agents of advice and support, but instead should try to understand how they fit into a complex support system. The doctor, teacher and psychologist may give the mother detailed advice and instruction, but her willingness or ability to put this into action may be more influenced by the views of her family, the needs of other members, the resources available and the range of support from her informal network or other professionals (Gottlieb, 1981).

From another perspective, the way the professional views the family is equally important. The rhetoric 'a handicapped child means a handicapped family' was useful in drawing attention to family needs and away from a child-focused framework. In doing so, however, it covertly implied an inevitable pathology for the family with a handicapped member. This has been reinforced by much research and practice which has been aimed at finding out pathologies in order to ameliorate them. Much clinical work has a similar emphasis, because it is predominantly crisis oriented and reactive to families with problems. Like textbooks or lectures which select cases and photographs that clearly illustrate the main characteristics of a condition or problem, this can tend to impart an extreme view which is then construed as the norm. Since our construct system directs our observations and deductions, this pathological orientation can result in professionals seeking out evidence to validate their views. This, together with the bias toward concentrating on families with extreme problems, is likely to reinforce extreme viewpoints and so the professional may fail to see the variety, individuality and normality within and between families. More importantly they may fail to seek out and acknowledge the family's competence in solving problems. As one mother commented, 'Why do they (professionals) always start by asking me if I have got any problems. Just because Mrs S——,' up the road can't cope . . .! My reaction is to say, "No" and to talk about the joys I have with David.'

It is understandable that parents may become defensive if they construe the emphasis of the professional as negative. To maintain a balance, the more negative the parent perceives professionals to be, the more likely they are to emphasize the positive. One consequence, which is almost universally noted by parents is that they are, or feel they are, labelled as non-accepting of the child's difficulty (see examples in Hewett, 1970; Hannam, 1980).

How should we interpret the case of parents attending a parents' evening for their 9 year old daughter? They were greeted with 'You really didn't need to come, she's getting in fine'. Does this imply that the teacher views contacts with the family as necessary only in the case of problems, or that family help is elicited only when teachers need it. In this case, the parents were very pleased and left with little discussion about the child's work. At home, they were greeted by the expectant child with 'What did she say? Did she say I was good? Did you see my writing – my display?' The parents could not answer for they had not seen the work. An opportunity was lost for reinforcing the child's competence and opening a discussion between child and parents of strong mutual interest. An opportunity was also lost for reinforcing parent actions in that the display had been influenced by a previous family outing. We must ask to what extent the three partners, the child, the teacher or the parents construed the purpose of the meeting from a problem orientation.

Families of children with special needs were just ordinary families before the child became a member (Seligman, 1983). They remain ordinary families, more alike than unlike other families, and their reactions should be seen as normal and typical. They are often subject to greater stress, because of increased caring needs and because of the greater variability of such children. This is illustrated articulately by Featherstone (1981). Like all of us, the family is confused by what to expect and hence what to do. This confusion should not automatically be interpreted as devoid of reality, as can happen when one combines a pathological and homogeneous framework so that all such families are inevitably assumed to have problems which are similar. It is, in fact, a reflection of reality. The use of such frameworks carries with it the danger that common parenting issues, such as how much freedom to give the child and how much control to exercise, can be misconstrued as overprotection, denial and rejection. In cases where the child's difficulties may be hypothesized to emanate from parenting factors, there is a danger of seeking out too quickly and failing to consider other factors which may be implicated, such as limited material resources or understanding. If the professional (or parent) construes all family problems and stress as emanating from the child's presence, they are more likely to conclude, for example, that the solution is the removal of the child or the need for treatment for the child.

If one accepts that families are highly variable with a range of individual needs and resources, then services must have a high degree of flexibility to meet these. Families with a child with severe intellectual impairment, for example, are faced with a life-time of involvement centred on the day-to-day care and management of the child. The child's difficulties are not remediable and therefore a short, extensive effort with a predictable time-span is not as applicable as it is to a family dealing with a reading problem or a behaviour disorder. Families are also ever-changing systems constantly adjusting to alterations in the number of members, resources, changing needs of members as they grow and develop, and changes in the extended network of relatives and friends. The latter is very apparent in step-families where there may be several family groups exerting a varying range of influences on family members (Carter & McGoldrick, 1980; Burgoyne & Clarke, 1984). Each family evolves its own methods and pattern for dealing with everyday demands, and professionals must be aware of the factors and processes related to this. Only then can they judge how they can best fit into the support network, set up the partnership and be of assistance. If they take this approach and apply a preventive model, they are more likely to search for strengths in the family, reinforce competence and develop strategies for meeting forseen difficulties.

The Family as a System

Recent attempts to understand how and why families work have suggested that it is useful to construe families as a system. Any system is made up of parts which work together for some shared purpose or common function. It can be analysed in terms of a structure and function and the processes by which the parts influence each other. In order to maintain itself and function, the system will have a set of needs and require resources to meet these. If there are changes in the structure, function or internal processes, adjustments must take place. If the resources can meet these changes, the system will maintain a reasonable balance and will function. From this viewpoint, a family which has sufficient resources to carry out the necessary activities to meet individual and family needs can function without undue stress. The use of a systems model of families, therefore, is an attempt to identify the ways and means that families use to maintain a balance or steady-state and to function in meeting needs of individual members (Olson & McCussin, 1983).

A number of family functions have been identified and not surprisingly are closely related to parenting and child needs discussed earlier. Ideally, the family provides economic and physical care, rest and leisure, and social and educational activities. It also provides affection and nurturance and an altruistic and concerned support group for its members. It acts as a model and reference group for discussion and learning, and will influence both interpersonal skills, and the core role structure of self-identity and values of its members.

As we noted earlier, the child's core role structure or self-identity initially develops within the family. Not only do children learn about themselves, they also learn about social norms and about what attributes are valued and encouraged or discouraged by the family. Later they will use their peer group and their extending and changing social networks to continue to develop and consolidate their core role structure. Thus, for example, children with physical impairments will usually learn gradually and within the family about their disability and the implications of being different. Siblings will learn to construe their brother's or sister's impairment from the family reaction to it. Studies have shown that siblings generally reflect the views of their parents. If the parents have made a healthy adjustment to the child's condition and convey this model in an open, honest interaction with the child and others, the siblings tend to adopt similar constructs and act accordingly. Hence the adjustment of the child to his/her own impairment and ways to deal with the reactions of others will initially depend largely upon the family model. Since many parents will not have learnt about a major disability gradually, but will have been confronted with an immediate shock and painful experience, they may use this to guide their anticipation of the child's future. They may then quite understandably try to protect the child from the anticipated pain. This may be disadvantageous to the child who will have to face these issues. Thus, the professional who understands the family system and the processes acting within it, may be able to share this with the parents and help them to recognize the process of adjustment in themselves and the child. This may then help them to anticipate future needs and so reduce the danger of crisis at some later date.

As the child with a physical impairment matures, he/she will have to develop more personal and independent views of him/herself and others. He/she will need to change his/her core role structure and construe him/herself from other people's points of view, as occurs in adolescence. The family will need to be aware of this and may require support in order to persevere and adapt to the child's needs at this time. As the child assumes emotional and social independence, the parents should gradually relinquish their responsibilities in this area. Indeed a function of the family will be to avoid inhibiting this growing independence by protecting the child too strongly or by reinforcing his/her dependence on the family.

Providing opportunities for the child to become independent is also likely to rest on resources such as time and money. The handicap may mean that considerable time in physical care is required, thus reducing the rest and leisure, or employment function of the parents. There appears to be increasing evidence that parents, especially mothers of severely handicapped children, do have reduced employment. Financial resources to deal with special equipment and mobility may also reduce what is available for other members. The social networks of other members may also be reduced because of lack of time, money or anticipation of how others will construe and react to the handicap.

The structure of the family can be seen in terms of (a) the numbers, age and sex of the members; (b) the roles that members take in the family, such as caretaking and decision making, and how they communicate and work together; and (c) the characteristics of the members. All have been noted as influencing the child with special needs and as being influenced by him/her. It is suggested, for example, that the larger the family, the less likely it is to be dominated by the child's difficulties. However, the larger the family, the greater can be the restraints on time, energy and finance.

There are so many factors operating within and on the family system, that it is not surprising that members spend a lot of energy maintaining the balance. Nor is it surprising that what may create a major strain in one family does not appear to upset another. One has to view the family system as a complex series of transactions, in which each element influences and is influenced by other elements. It is not really possible to make precise predictions about which factors are likely to have effects on particular families at particular times. Consequently, models of family structures or functioning can only give limited guidance about the range of factors that might be involved and how the professional can weight their likely importance in the context of a specific family system. With this in mind, the next section describes some of the major aspects which are helpful to consider. These relate to (i) the characteristics of the family; (ii) the effects on different members, e.g. fathers, mothers, and siblings; (iii) marital relationships and family harmony; (iv) the extended family and social networks; and (v) life-cycle events.

Characteristics of the Family

The type and degree of special need, appearance, sex, age, behavioural and temperamental factors have all been reported as influencing parental adjustment and family functioning (Glendinning, 1983; De Meyers, 1979; Miezio, 1983; Kew, 1975; Gregory, 1976). It has been suggested, for example, that parents are less stressed by having a daughter with special needs, than a son. This may be due to traditional sex stereotypes influencing aspirations, with girls being seen as fitting in with domestic arrangements and being more dependent than boys. Equally, it is suggested that conditions with marked physical appearance can be more distressing for parents of girls than boys. Changing social attitudes to sex and appearance will presumably influence such reactions.

Age is often cited as important. As the child gets older so more stress is often found, and the level of satisfaction with the parenting role can reduce. This is often related to life-cycle events and the increasing independence of the child (see below). As the child grows, for example, and becomes more mobile and independent, he/she will demand more freedom to extend activities beyond the immediate household. This increases the amount of supervisory time needed and entails decisions about how much freedom to give, which will be dependent upon the local environment. Parents who have a large garden, or live in a quiet cul-de-sac or close to recreational facilities, may be more able to allow the child greater freedom of movement.

Another likely source of stress relates to the age of the child and concerns the parent's increasing awareness of the nature or degree of the child's handicap, and its implications for the child and family. Similarly, any behavioural difficulties or control and management problems become more influential. This may also relate to increased stress reported with boys, who tend to display more behavioural management problems. For both sexes, the onset of puberty is likely to cause some stress with different consequences for boys and girls.

The level of intellectual impairment is often assumed to be highly related to stress in families. There is, however, no straightforward link between these, and some recent studies have not found this to be the case. Rather, it is the demands made by the child upon the family resources which are related to stress. For example, the need for physical care and medical/health problems, will reduce the time that individual members and the family have as a whole for other activities. It may also influence work by restricting both mother and father and so have an effect on financial resources. Hence, in so far as intellectual impairment reduces the level of the child's independent functioning, e.g. in personal care and self-help skills, demands are increased. However, physical or sensory impairments can have similar results. Management demands due to behavioural difficulties again influence economic, leisure and vocational functioning, as well as cause disruption in daily routines. It is generally found that the unpredictability of the child's behaviour is amongst the most common sources of stress. If parents cannot anticipate/construe the child's behaviour or needs, they will be extremely anxious and be unable to establish routines and organize the running of the family. Not only does this increase anxiety and tension within families, it also means spending a great deal of the family resources, in terms of energy and time, on supervisory caretaking.

Again, the relationship between parental anxiety and stress is not straightforward. For example, parents who have additional sources of stress, such as marital disharmony, often perceive behaviour difficulties as relatively greater than parents who do not. The degree of stress on the family, therefore, results from the interaction between the demands made by the child's difficulties and family resources.

Anxiety and satisfaction with parenting have also been linked with the level of the child's social responsiveness. Whilst this has been mainly demonstrated with young children with intellectual impairment, it is also seen in children who are withdrawn, and who do not express their feelings and concerns. Many parents testify to the frustration of not being able to get children to talk to them about the reasons for their behaviour. They describe feeling rejected or shut out by the child and of not experiencing affectionate reactions.

Effects Upon Different Family Members

Siblings

Research on siblings has often relied on questioning parents rather than the children. Since parents' views will be influenced by their hopes for their children and their perception of what has been 'given up' for the child with special needs, they often report more severe negative consequences than the siblings. Siblings are usually unaware of what might have been and report the positive advantages. Most siblings do not appear to be adversely affected and many reports note benefits such as increased tolerance and understanding toward others.

However, in large families and, particularly for elder sisters, the sibling may be placed in a caretaking role and have to assume a degree of parental responsibility for the child with special needs or younger siblings (Gath, 1978). This can limit the opportunities for personal development and extending social relationships. Some evidence suggests that this can also result in emotional disturbance, which appears to be more likely in the case of severe physical or behavioural difficulties. In other words, disturbance is more likely when the demands on the family stretch resources to the extent that a reasonable balance can only be maintained by using resources which should function to provide for the needs of other members. Seen in this way, the risk to siblings is preventable and not inevitable. It requires a spread of caretaking roles, which might come from the informal social network, such as grandparents, or from the services.

Siblings can also experience difficulties from the reactions of friends and other children, such as teasing or harsh comments about the brother or sister. It appears that this has only a temporary effect when the family generally construes the child positively and is open and honest in discussion. More difficult are the recurring occasions when they have to explain their brother's or sister's behaviour to others. This may be associated with feelings of embarrassment or protectiveness and, consequently, they may require advice and information on how to deal with it.

For many siblings, knowledge about the impairment is important, because they may fear that they will 'catch the disability' or that there is future risk to their own children. Several studies indicate that many siblings are rather ignorant of the details of causes, and that they do not raise these issues with their parents.

Generally the more understandable and/or more socially acceptable the special need, the less the anxiety is felt by siblings, and indeed by all the family members. However, the social acceptability of the handicap will be influenced by both cultural and societal values and the personal values of the family. For example, where families value intellectual performance, learning difficulties may be less acceptable, and they may find it more difficult to adjust.

There is also a lack of information about why some families fail to provide the support and knowledge to allay sibling anxiety. Some studies have reported that siblings feel they cannot react negatively toward their brother or sister with special needs. This appears to be unacceptable to parents, who encourage more positive activities such as playing with and helping the child. Few parents, however, would not try to discourage sibling rivalry and aggression, whether or not their children have special needs. It is difficult, therefore, to determine whether this inhibition of 'negative' expression of feelings is construed differently because of the child's handicap or whether it reflects a strong protective feeling in the family. If the sibling construes that parents find it painful and embarrassing to talk about the child's handicap it may inhibit them from asking questions. It has also been suggested that where parents have difficulty adjusting to their child's problem and have high aspirations for their children, some siblings may feel the need to compensate for parental disappointment by overachieving.

Finally, there is inconclusive evidence that in small families, siblings who are younger or near the same age as the child with special needs may be at risk of disturbance. Again, this appears to be related to the degree to which the demands made by the child restrict the daily interactions between the parents and other children, and the resources of the family. For reviews of research with siblings of handicapped children see Simeonsson & McHale (1981) and Lobato (1983).

Fathers

Some studies report that fathers are more affected by a disability in the child and take longer to adjust than mothers. It is suggested that this is because men are more achievement oriented and more concerned with the development of attainments and independence in their children. It is also suggested that the birth of a child with an impairment is a greater shock to the core role structure and self-esteem of fathers, because it is largely based on sociocultural values such as manhood, independence, competitiveness and achievement. Again one might anticipate changes in such reactions, as stereotyped sex roles change. An alternative explanation, however, may be that services tend to deal with mothers, who have more frequent access to appropriate support networks (e.g. other mothers at clinics and schools) and may be more prepared for the possibility of an impairment, because of their broader experience of child care. In this case the mother enters the process of adjustment at a different stage and receives different support. Thus the difficulties found with some fathers may relate to resources rather than assumed genetotypical factors.

A similar explanation can be extended to the findings that fathers' involvement with children increases with the age of the child. This does appear to be changing as male-female roles alter in some cultures. Fathers' involvement is found to differ across socio-cultural backgrounds, but generally more fathers of children with intellectual impairments are involved with care activities than fathers of ordinary children. There is some indication, however, that fathers are less likely to spend time with the child, the more he/she is developmentally delayed. Once again, this may reflect a lack of experience and knowledge of young children, and there is some evidence that father's involvement does increase if encouraged and given constructive guidance of ways to handle or help the child. This may also reduce the need for families to use residential care, as this is correlated with low father participation in child care activities.

There is some evidence that fathers may be less aware than mothers of the degree of strain the child's demands make on the family and may also have a less optimistic view than mothers of the child's current and future attainments. Another difference is that fathers appear more likely to take on an assertive role to fight for family rights and express demands when dealing with services. This role differentiation, of mothers dealing with daily care and internal family interactions, and fathers with external interactions, may well be a practical strategy for maintaining balance. Yet, father's assertiveness, low expectations or unwillingness to acknowledge stresses, has been interpreted as 'non-acceptance', as a blow to self-esteem and manhood.

Alternatively, and perhaps more constructively, such findings can be explained by the necessity for fathers to go out to work and for mothers to be largely responsible for day-to-day care. Consequently, fathers have less time to assume the day-to-day care role and to observe the emerging behaviours and changes in the child. They may be more outward oriented and perceive that their energies are best used in fighting for the child's rights and interacting with professionals at critical times such as in selection of school provision. Their daily interactions through work may also provide them with more confidence and skill in dealing with professionals. On the other hand, mothers may by necessity have to take a more inward orientation within the family, using their skills and energies in day-to-day care and maintenance of the system, and they may thus feel less able to deal with professional services at these critical times.

Whatever differences are seen in these studies, it is important not to jump too quickly to interpretations based upon inevitable consequences of sex roles or of fathers' emotional difficulties. It is also worth noting that differences may alter considerably with changes in society and family roles, and when the provision of support includes fathers. Many of these issues are reviewed in

Beail & McGuire (1982) and particularly in a chapter dealing with fathers of mentally handicapped children (McConachie, 1982).

Mothers

Nevertheless, current research findings do show that mothers shoulder the main day-to-day care and are more likely to experience both physical and emotional strain (Wilkins, 1979). The main difficulties for mothers often relate to parenting issues and feelings of competence. It is suggested that this is due to mothers being more inward looking and concerned with the emotional wellbeing of the family as well as the fact that they spend so much time with the child.

One frequently noted difficulty is the feeling of isolation. This relates to the social restriction placed on mothers and is associated with younger children and with the severity of demands made by the child with special needs. However, social isolation and loneliness are not restricted to young families. More severely handicapped people are living in the community and, like all people, are living longer. Many parents are therefore entering their later years with dependent children for whom they must care. Given the restrictions of mobility, social contact and economic restraints, that are more common to older people, then isolation and loneliness crosses all age ranges. Unlike the mother of the young child, many of these parents do not have access to a wide social network, through, for example, taking the child to school. Indeed, for many families, particularly if one spouse has died or is also infirm, isolation is a major concern. Often the handicapped son or daughter provides company as well as making a major contribution to running the household, and strong bonds of mutual help and dependency exist.

There is also a sense of isolation in that fathers and mothers can believe their position is not understood by society. In such cases the social network is particularly important for reducing physical and psychological isolation.

Marital Relationships and Family Harmony

It is often argued that the incidence of marital break-up and family disharmony is higher in families with severely handicapped children. The evidence, however, is far from conclusive, and the incidence varies with such factors as the age of the child and the nature of the child's handicap (Friedrich & Freidrich, 1981). Studies indicate that marital satisfaction decreases over time in all kinds of families and not just in those with handicapped children. Whether there is a disproportional decrease in relation to the increasing demands made by the child's handicap is not yet known. When representative samples of families are surveyed, many studies find that most marriages remain intact (e.g. Kazak & Marvia, 1984). It is frequently noted that separation and disharmony are more likely when there have been prior marital difficulties. It also appears that typical family controversies over caretaking demands, disagreements about discipline and management, future needs and expectations are accentuated by the child's special needs, since they take place in the context of higher uncertainty and demands. This is supported by the finding that, although there are no major differences in overall frequency of marital breakdown, measures of both positive and negative aspects of harmony are more extreme, with, for example, an apparent strengthening of the relationship when there was strong harmony before the diagnosis (e.g. Gath, 1978). However, marital relationships are vulnerable to the demands of day-to-day care and the increasing demands on family resources as children grow older. By implication, disharmony should be reduced if support is given to lessen other stresses, and recent research tentatively suggests this may be so. Since the marital relationship is at the heart of many families, it is an important area for professional concern.

Families with good organization, overtly or covertly agreed role differentiation, open expressiveness and decision making, and cohesion, appear less vulnerable to strain or stress (e.g. Mink et al., 1983). Mothers who feel secure in their relationship and parenting role also appear to have fewer signs of stress, such as ill-health or feeling unwell, dissatisfied and low in self-confidence.

Social Networks and the Extended Family

The extended family and the more general social network offers practical assistance with day-to-day care, such as child minding, transport and the provision of material resources. Also it can provide support in the form of a reference group, which parents can use to appraise their ways of construing events and their actions.

Some recent evidence indicates that families of children with severe impairments tend to have smaller, more dense, social networks, which appear to foster a sense of cohesiveness and support, but which may also produce different stresses (e.g. Kuzak & Marvin, 1984). It may, for example, result in a concentration of resources on activities related to the impairment. If parents feel that others have a negative view of them and their child, they may avoid such social contacts and prefer the safety of the family circle and small social network. This may then restrict opportunities for social activities and for developing broader frames of reference which provide alternative views.

Conversely, the interaction with broader networks and social values can cause family members to question their feelings toward the child and whether their efforts are justified. Such questioning is bound to increase their uncertainties and may influence their interactions with the child and other family members. If different family members have different views and/or are influenced by different social networks with different attitudes and norms, it may cause conflict. Indeed the enduring problem for many families is the maintenance of positive ways of construing the child within a society that generally values intellectual and physical achievement. As the child gets older and the implications of the handicap become more apparent and society's reactions more pertinent and instrumental, so parental anxieties can increase. Consequently, the views and actions of the immediate neighbourhood are important. Parents who feel that the neighbours understand are more able to give their child freedom to play and move about the immediate neighbourhood, which not only offers wider experiences for the child, but also some freedom from supervisory activities, or as one another put it, 'A little time for myself'.

Relationships with the extended family and social networks vary enormously and are influenced by cultural and geographic factors. Professional, middle-class people more often have widely dispersed extended families and this reduces the amount of day-to-day contact and provision of immediate help. The telephone, however, can provide access to psychological support, but such families also tend to value individual attainment and independence and parents do not wish to place constraints on older siblings or close relatives.

Where the extended family network is within a close geographic location, active help may be more available. However, it is often the female members of the family who take on the main responsibilities for daily care. There is also a differentiation of caring roles, with parents assuming responsibility for the personal care of the child (e.g. dressing and feeding) with members of the wider social network helping with such areas as shopping or child minding. This is largely controlled by the parents' view of what is right or reasonable to expect of others and the willingness of others to comply. Hence, families even though they are under great strain, may be unwilling to relinquish certain areas of care. This is very much controlled by their constructions of themselves and their roles (i.e. core role structure) and the guilt (as defined earlier) that arises from not meeting one's own expectations. Circumstances that arise to prevent them meeting what they construe as their responsibilities may lead to considerable disturbances, which must be helped by careful attention to the necessity for changes to take place in their construct system.

On a broader level, if parents construe that society does not value their child and by implication, the efforts they carry out to help the child, then they face a persistent challenge and potential invalidation of their construct system. This may make them particularly sensitive to any suggestion of devaluation of their child and/or themselves, with the reaction, as discussed earlier, of balancing the negative by being more publicly positive than they really feel.

The professional must not only be aware of the nature of support families receive from the informal social networks, they must also be sensitive to any changes in the network and anticipate whether extra strain will result and how adjustments can be made. In helping parents to make these adjustments they will need to be aware of how the family construe their responsibilities, aims and values. It is unlikely to be helpful for the professional to state indignantly that other members of the support network should be giving more help, without a careful consideration of the families' way of making sense of themselves. In order to begin to help, the professional must understand that families are changing systems constantly adjusting to internal and external difficulties.

Life-Cycle Events: Changes and Adjustments

At different times families experience rapid periods of change and growth and at other times relative stability. Again such changes relate to the structure and function of the family. How these changes are brought about will depend upon the processes used by the family to communicate, make decisions, and to work together. Often the changes are related to life-cycle events such as the birth of a child, children going to or leaving school, or leaving home. These are transition points which have complex effects within the system. For example, when a child goes to school, families have to make decisions about such issues as the type of school and travel arrangements, which may require re-organization of roles and routines. It often means a time for reappraisal of their construct system. For families with a severely handicapped child this is frequently a period of great searching.

Should they select a special school? Should they accept or reject professional advice? If they reject it, is it because they have not fully adjusted to, or comprehended, the extent of the child's handicap? Are they fearful of the stigma that may be attached? If they accept special schooling will other family members, siblings and relatives, cope with any perceived stigma? Are they doing the best for the child or are they being selfish in that the special school provides door-to-door transport? Are they being too protective?

In turn, once mothers no longer have young dependent children, they can consider whether to return to work and pursue a career. This will involve them in (i) the process of reconstruing themselves in relation to the family; (ii) a balancing of family and personal needs; and (iii) a restructuring of roles in terms of daily routines which will effect all family members. The extra financial benefits may alter decision-making roles concerned with how money is spent, and there may be a reduction in the time that the husband can spend on his work or all family members can spend in recreation.

Such situations are obviously associated with high uncertainty, and the evaluation of relative disadvantages and advantages has to be largely subjective. In general, these situations will involve anxiety. However, provided families have healthy processes for interaction and reasonable consensus of values and aspirations, they usually adjust. If, on the other hand, they are under pressure from other sources, such as caring for a child with special needs, the addition of further anxiety may be overwhelming.

Whilst a particular change in family circumstances may precipitate a crisis, in most cases adverse effects are usually found not from one source of stress alone, but when several sources combine to overcome family or individual resources. It is for this reason that those involved with family support require a framework to provide an insight into the multifaceted system of the family (Seligman, 1983; Blacher, 1984). One should not, however, feel overwhelmed by the complexity. Many families function well with relatively little professional input. Often a particular source of stress can be recognized and dealing with it prevents major disruption in the system. The role of the professional is to work with parents to help them to identify and anticipate (i) needs or sources of stress, (ii) the resources which are required to meet these, and (iii) strategies to ensure the resources are available.

Needs and Resources

Previously, special needs were defined not in traditional categories of disability, but in such areas as mobility, financial assistance, specialized information, special education or treatment and so on. They are in fact the special resources needed by the family and its members to maintain a balanced system. If there is an imbalance between the demands placed on the system and the resources, then one can expect strain or stress. Hence a source of stress is synonymous with a lack of resources, and needs are statements of actual or expected resources to maintain a balance and prevent stress. The maintainance of this balance is necessary for family well-being and functioning. As noted earlier, functioning includes the aims and aspirations of the family and so stress is related to the extent that these are met. Since different families have different aims and aspirations, as well as variations in resources, it is not surprising that apparently similar demands can result in different degrees of stress and different ways of adapting.

Adaptation clearly implies the need for change, either in the way the family system functions and/or in the construct systems of the family members. As discussed in earlier chapters, emotions such as threat and anxiety are defined in terms of the awareness of the need for change. The ways that are used to deal with such anxiety and stress are called coping strategies. Thus denial of the diagnosis of a handicap can be seen as a coping strategy to reduce the anxiety or stress resulting from the imbalance between one's construct system and the implications of the diagnosis. Similarly, providing the parents with financial help, information or access to a self-help group are all coping strategies to reduce stress from caretaking demands, uncertainty and feelings of isolation respectively.

This is a problem-solving activity which seeks to define the sources of stress, in relation to family functioning and the strategies to make resources available. This framework can apply to personal changes of family members and to the family as a whole. Personal strategies may involve, for example, learning new skills and exploring reactions and feelings, whilst family strategies will concern such areas as interrelationships, organizing caretaking and maintaining a balance between resources coming into the family (e.g. finances) and the function of the family in providing for individual needs.

The aim, however, is not just to help families cope, but to facilitate family well-being and functioning. There is a danger in interpreting 'coping' in a limited and negative way of 'just getting by'. This can lead to a crisis-oriented approach with the focus on minimal levels of family functioning rather than on an admittedly more idealistic aim, of improving the quality of life for all family members. The latter view is less likely to lead professionals into suggesting that they are only interested in working with families if there is a problem.

Since needs and resources are so closely related, we will discuss a general classification of resources before concluding with the needs of parents with a special child.

Resources

Current frameworks for analysing resources generally refer to five main categories (e.g. Folkman et al., 1979):

(1) Utilitarian Resources   These include finance, mobility, energy saving devices, respite care, housing, specialist equipment and toys. Often, especially when applying a pathological orientation, the importance of utilitarian resources is overlooked. Many parents argue they would function very well if these resources were available, but when they are not, a spiral of fatigue and stress results with knock-on effects for relationships and family processes. An extreme, but poignant example might be that for many years there has been a tendency to blame poor school attainment, adjustment and attitudes of children from low socio-economic groups on parental attitudes and behaviour, when most may emanate from the lack of utilitarian resources. Similarly, there is some tentative evidence that stress is more likely to be associated with socio-economic status than with the degree of intellectual impairment.

(2) Health and Energy Levels   This includes both physical and psychological wellbeing. We noted earlier that mothers of physically demanding children are more likely to suffer health difficulties. Similarly, parents seeking help for behavioural difficulties of children are more likely to have additional emotional problems. Low energy will result in reduced capacity for daily activities and problem solving.

(3) Problem-Solving Skills   This refers to the ability and experience in finding solutions to problems. Parents who have high level skills in seeking out and understanding information and utilizing sources of support are more likely to develop appropriate strategies. They are more likely to feel competent and act independently. Hence, early parent support, which reinforces parent competence and also demonstrates how they might use and trust professional services, is important in reducing the future likelihood of stress.

(4) Support Networks   As discussed earlier, this refers to relationships between individuals or families and others who provide (i) emotional support; (ii) a reference group for guidance and con-

firmation through discussion and comparison; and (iii) utilitarian assistance and practical support.

(5) Philosophy   We would translate this directly to mean the individual's construct system. As a parent, how one construes one's own competence and problem-solving skills, one's beliefs and values in relation to the family and parenting, the sort of children one wants, and anticipations and desires for the future are all important resources or influences on reducing stress and maintaining functioning. Each member of the family will have their own construct system. Depending on the interactions between members there will be a set of shared family beliefs and values. The degree of consensus in the family construct system will influence the harmony and joint decision-making process and can be seen as a resource for maintenance and change.

Needs

As we have argued, needs are expected resources related to family functioning. For clarification they can be categorized, but they are part of a transactional system and highly interrelated. They fall into two main categories, practical assistance and psychological support. Practical assistance can be further sub-divided into utilitarian needs and instrumental needs. Utilitarian needs are related to the time and energy that the family or individual members have for personal or family functions. The less time and energy spent on basic home management and caretaking, the more that is available for recreation and social activities and involvement with the children.

Families may require assistance in travel, energy saving devices, respite care, holiday facilities, access to community facilities, such as clubs, parks and swimming pools, and financial assistance. Such needs are more likely to be required where children make considerable demands on resources due to medical, physical or behavioural difficulties and/or for low income families.

Instrumental needs are largely concerned with information and guidance on such areas as:

(i)   Organizing their time, energy, and finances.
(ii)   Ways of encouraging the child's development and attainment of skills. This should consider minimizing the time and energy required to achieve most benefit, if it is not to add stress.
(iii) Ways of managing behaviour difficulties.
(iv)   Information on obtaining social service provision, education facilities, recreational facilities, access to specialist

therapists and rights and allowances.
(v)   Guidance and training on personal communication skills
        in order to obtain rights and to work with service agencies.
        This may also extend to how to interact and deal with
        other people. For some this may include help in extending
        social networks and broadening contacts.

Psychological needs concern:–

(i)   Information to enable family members to understand the
        child and his/her condition, their own feelings and reac-
        tions and those of others and the processes of adjustment.
        This means the development of frameworks to make sense
        of their situation and anticipate and plan for future events.
        With respect to the child this must include access to medi-
        cal, developmental and educational knowledge. Particu-
        larly, it must include access to the diagnostic or assessment
        procedures on which decisions are based and inclusion
        in the decision-making process.
(ii)   Social support to prevent isolation and provide for leisure
        and recreation, utilitarian help, and an opportunity to com-
        pare one's own ideas and feelings to others and to thereby
        obtain new perspectives.

Concluding Comment

This chapter has attempted to provide a framework of family functioning to guide the professional's actions. What has been discussed is far from conclusive or definitive and reflects the lack
of investigation and information in this area and the complexity.
Clearly, not all aspects of the frameworks are critical to or relevant
to all families at all times. Indeed, the ever changing nature and
immense variation within and between families means that any
framework can never be more than a set of guiding principles.
Professionals have to use such frameworks to make the best and
most informed guesses they can, in order to analyse situations
competently and to suggest options and strategies for joint consideration. This must emphasize the competence of parents and
families and be useful in seeking practical, mutually acceptable
goals and solutions. All families faced with a child with special
needs will require relevant information and guidance which is
accurate and practical. Central to this is information which helps
them to understand and make sense of the child's behaviour and
their own behaviour. Most will require some form of psychological

CHAPTER 6

Using Counselling Skills

As stated in Chapter 1, the term counselling refers to any situation between two people, in which one construes the other as having relevant competence and willingness to assist, and the other has the intention to do so. Therefore, counselling exists when the speech therapist communicates the results of a language assessment or the occupational therapist advises on a mobility aid. It might be potentially more dramatic where the paediatrician is communicating a severe diagnosis. It occurs where a teacher is advising the parents on how to deal with a behaviour problem, or where the psychologist is helping the parents to resolve a marital crisis.

Whether the parents are seen once by an audiologist or on a continuing basis by the teacher, whatever their specialized knowledge, whatever their purpose in relating to parents, whatever the severity of the problem, the professional is interacting with parents and is counselling. We have argued earlier that many of these skills are basic to social interaction and professionals have them. However, the pity is that they may lack confidence in the use of these skills, be unaware of them or the process of counselling, or construe that they should act differently in a professional capacity as compared to a personal situation.

In general, therefore, professionals should have two major areas of competence. The first is concerned with their own professional discipline (e.g. teaching, medicine, social work). The second is the ability to communicate this competence, and involves counselling skills. This chapter is concerned with the acquisition and refinement of these skills and with the provision of a framework for thinking about the process of counselling. For more detailed information about counselling skills generally, refer to Egan (1981) and Nelson-Jones (1983). For further information about counselling parents of children with special needs see Seligman (1979) and Webster (1977).

The intention is to consider (i) the aims and functions of counselling; (ii) its skills and characteristics and (iii) the stages in the process. Before this, however, a word of warning is necessary. As with all skilled performance, what the professional does at any moment is not guided by fixed and rigid rules. Specific actions must be dependent upon the circumstances existing at the time. Minute planning cannot occur, nor can anything that is said in this chapter be absolute. Counselling is a function of the ways the individuals involved, professional and parents, construe each other and their relationship. Nevertheless, there are principles and guidelines that can be described. By nature these amount to a simplification of what is a very complex set of events. Therefore, what are considered important factors for successful outcome are more like informed guesses than certain prediction. Whatever the content of parent–professional interactions, this chapter will consider the general process. However, since a major theme in this work will be the attempt to change children's behaviour, the use of behaviour modification is an important part of the repertoire for all professionals. Using a behavioural model to analyse a child's behaviour can be extremely useful, when other explanations are either unavailable or have failed to suggest ways of helping. The techniques, used extensively to good effect, have been described in detail in many places (Wheldall & Merrett, 1984; Yule & Carr, 1980). As mentioned earlier, the behavioural model is not incompatible with a framework based upon Personal Construct Theory, since it is a set of constructs that can be placed upon events in order to make them meaningful in the sense of anticipating what should be done in relation to them. Although much use can be made of behavioural methods, they are not an automatic and mechanical solution to learning difficulties. They have to be seen within the total picture of counselling, one outcome of which may be their use.

Aims and Functions of Counselling

It is important to begin by discussing the aims of counselling, because by establishing the aims:

(i)   The counselling is given direction.
(ii) The direction can be shared and discussed with the family.

(iii)   The process can be evaluated in terms of whether the aims have been achieved.

General Aims

Although by negotiation the professional must consider and set explicit aims for intervention with each family separately and to revise them as necessary, there are three general aims.

1. *Usefulness*   At the most general level the aim is *to be useful* to the family. Usefulness is not only to be judged in terms of the professional's views, but in terms of the needs as *the family perceives them*. The professional must be aware of what the parents want and must assess whether the helping process is meeting these needs. If there is a discrepancy between the perceived aims of the parents and those of the professional, then this must be identified, discussed and hopefully resolved. Further, the professional should then closely monitor whether the parents perceive the counselling as useful. If necessary this should be done by explicit and direct enquiry. Although it may be embarrassing, the ability to say, for example, 'Is that what you expected?' or 'Has that been helpful?' is essential in order to minimize misunderstandings on either side.

2. *Adaptation*   A most important aim is to facilitate the adaptation of the family as a whole, so that all members function effectively. Even when the professional is imparting information in the first and only contact with the family, they should still be aware that skilful and sensitive interaction is necessary to facilitate adaptation and not hinder it. This means helping them to understand their situation, to adapt to it by making the most of what confronts them currently and enable them to strive to make realistic improvements. It does not mean making everything right for them, but helping them to make their situation as right as it can be. Again exact aims are dependent upon the individual family, their abilities, their resources and the context in which they live. The rich family with two children and the single parent struggling to feed four children require very different approaches. What is important, however, is to achieve a balance between the needs of all the family members. It is not uncommon for most resources to be focused upon a child with special needs to the neglect of other people in the family. This may be regarded as adaptive if all the family are happy with such a situation, but it may be damaging if, for example, the needs of a spouse or other children are not considered by open discussion.

3. *Development of Constructs*   In terms of the theory discussed in

Chapter 3, adaptation is dependent upon the construct system that is available to parents (i.e. the framework they have for making sense of what is happening around them and to them). Only by having a usable construct system will the parents be able to anticipate what is likely to happen and, in consequence, be able to adjust effectively. Therefore, the aim is to help in and speed up the development of a workable, useful construct system. Help is provided to the extent that the process of rebuilding is facilitated and not hindered. *The ideal outcome of counselling, therefore, is for parents to construe themselves as having been effective in dealing with their situation by their own efforts and to feel able to face the future without, or with limited professional help.*

Basic Functions

Four major functions have been identified for the sake of clarity, but these are highly interrelated.

1. *Support*   Whenever a person is confronted by a significant problem, they may benefit by support from others. A basic function of counselling, therefore, is to provide just this support. This involves caring for the family, respecting them and tolerating them, even when they might expect to be disliked or rejected. It means doing nothing to add to their present difficulties by making them feel inferior or by reducing their self-esteem. It means not only being available when necessary, but also helping the parents to understand their own existing social support system and how their actions could endanger this by alienating others.

The function of support as envisaged here is not merely to provide a buttress for people who may be in a weak state. Rather, it is to allow parents to explore their situation fully and to experiment in various ways so that they may obtain a better understanding of what they face and, therefore, become more effective in dealing with it. This may allow a breathing space and prevent them from acting precipitately and committing themselves prematurely. Crisis by its nature motivates people to seek immediate solutions. Since these may not be available or may be dependent upon careful deliberation, the opportunity for thought is important. Professionals may actually forewarn the parents that they should not make an immediate decision until their next meeting. Similarly, they may need to advise parents against making dogmatic statements. For example, the statement 'He will be going to the normal school', might lead to a discussion of the uncertainty of the future as well as the difficulties added by such a public declaration if later they have to contradict themselves.

If one offers and provides support to a family, careful attention must be given to how it is withdrawn. Since the recipient of the support is ultimately the only person to know when they no longer need the support, then a negotiated withdrawal is required. This should not be done suddenly, but, for example, by arranging to meet for one or two more sessions to enable discussion of the implications. In fact, this illustrates a general principle of *forewarning parents of change*. Even in an individual session, it is important to indicate when it is likely to finish and to warn the parents ten minutes or so before the end, that the professional must leave shortly. This is useful, because parents often bring up significant issues at the end of the session. The professional needs time to discuss these even if it means deciding to defer the issue until the next meeting. If parents perceive professionals as 'rushing off' just at the important point, then they may construe them as 'not really interested' or 'too busy to be bothered'. In general, where possible, an individual session should best be ended at a high point, where the parents feel they have been supported.

2. *Information Provision*   A basic function of counselling is either to provide information for the parents or to direct them to where relevant information may be obtained. When parents ask questions, professionals should be able to answer directly or obtain answers subsequently. This will range from questions about the physical or psychological causes of the child's difficulty, to help that is available and the long-term consequences. Accurate and comprehensive information is needed to establish a realistic appraisal of present and future situations.

Providing information does not simply mean telling parents all that professionals think they should know. They have to judge what information might be required, but it is ultimately the parent who must be the judge. The professional must begin by finding out the parent's current knowledge and immediate questions, and then indicate other areas of information that they might need. This will often relate to information outside the parent's experience, but which will be of eventual value in preventing future difficulty. For example, parents with young children who are severely handicapped may have adjusted to the initial trauma, but they need to be warned that such feelings can return later.

Providing information is no guarantee that it will be understood and remembered. Parents given a full explanation of their child's brain damage may deny, even within a few hours, that they have been given such information. Very often they do not remember, because when given bad news the turmoil or shock prevents them from attending to what is being said. On the other hand, they may not remember, because the person who was imparting the information did not communicate it in an appropriate way. The relevance of the information may not be clear, because the parents do not have the appropriate construct system to make sense of the information at this time. The professional should, therefore, check that they have understood what has been said and recheck their understanding in later sessions.

Since counsellors are not omniscient, there will be times when they are not able to provide answers. There will also be occasions when there is *no* answer. In the former case the professional should discuss the best source of the required help with the parents, so that they may be referred to the most appropriate agency. Where possible the counselling should include the available options and services, which the parents should be helped to evaluate and utilize. Referral to another professional does not mark the end of the counselling relationship, since the family may need help to make sense of the results of the referral. In the latter case, the professional should make it quite clear that there are no absolute answers. If the issue, for example, is about the cause of the child's difficulties, then it should be explained that there is no way of knowing. However, the professional should discuss with the parents what would be the value of such information if it were available. Similarly, in predicting future developments, the professional should share the difficulties involved in making such predictions.

3. *Facilitate Change*   When discussing the general objectives we emphasized the importance of helping the parents to adapt and to develop an adequate system of constructs. A major function of the counselling, therefore, is to help parents to change, both in the ways they view their world and in the ways they behave. This may occur by supporting them and by providing them with information. However, there may be occasions when counsellors may force the pace. They may challenge the views of the parents or provide them with an alternative model. It is at this point that professionals are closest to adopting a more dominant position, though they still need sensitivity and the ability to communicate skilfully and carefully. This raises the ever present dilemma of knowing when to push and when to hold back. For example, if it is felt that the parents are 'unrealistic' about the child's ability or 'do not accept the handicap', this means that they are not construing the child in the same way as the professional. Who is to say who is correct, but does it matter at this stage, since the goal is to arrive at ways of facilitating useful change? When the professional challenges a parental view, it is helpful if both con-

strue the parental situation as a state of transition where they are rebuilding their construct system. *The aim is to test the usefulness of alternative ways of construing, rather than finding definitive answers.* Being told that they are denying reality is unlikely to facilitate change, whereas challenging their constructs with the view that, like the professional, they are themselves involved in a scientific pursuit, making hypotheses and testing them, may be meaningful.

4. *Training* The final function of counselling is to teach or train the parents in the skills they need in order to deal actively with their situation. The task is to help them change their understanding as discussed above, and also to change their behaviour to help them acquire appropriate skills. This might involve, for example, teaching them to observe their children accurately, or teaching behavioural skills or even training them to use counselling techniques. For example, role-play can be used with parents in order to teach them how to listen to others effectively. Such skills could enrich their interactions with their children and other adults, including professionals. Certainly the emphasis in recent years has been upon training parents to use behavioural techniques (see Chapter 7) with many books being written to help them (e.g. Cunningham & Sloper, 1978; Carr, 1980).

In doing this the professional is *sharing his/her psychological knowledge and skills.* To do so may be valuable, because it may enhance the parents' feelings of self-efficacy, self-esteem and self-responsibility. These skills may, therefore, enhance their ability to function on their own. It is of limited value if professionals only use their own skills whilst supporting the family. This is likely to foster dependence and feelings of inadequacy. It is preferable for parents to be able to tackle immediate problems themselves and to be able to resolve future problems as they are presented.

Counselling Characteristics and Skills

With these functions in mind, we will consider counselling characteristics that will maximize successful outcome. As noted in Chapter 1, parents' criticisms concerned (i) professional competence, (ii) the ability to communicate and (iii) personal qualities. To demonstrate competence the professional needs to be equipped with the set of major frameworks already discussed: a model of the parent–professional relationship; a model of individual functioning; a model of family functioning. Additionally, they will have their own professional expertise, with a knowledge of child development and children with special needs. It is also useful to have a detailed knowledge of local and national resources.

The ability to communicate and to demonstrate appropriate personal qualities are highly interrelated, but for purposes of clarity we will focus upon key aspects.

1. Respect

As with many of the characteristics to be discussed, we have to consider not only what the professional believes and feels, but also what he/she communicates to the family. Respect is the belief that the family are valuable and important. This implies not only that professionals are prepared to give help willingly, but also that they believe that the family can cope, can change and can be strong. It implies an absolute faith in the parents' expertise, their ability to make decisions and to be responsible for themselves. This is not a belief about the future after counselling, but about the family immediately; *they are, not they will be.* Perhaps the shortest way of summarizing this is to use Carl Roger's term of unconditional positive regard (i.e. to regard the family positively without attaching conditions). Its importance for the process of counselling lies in our belief that people *receive help more readily and may change when they feel they are giving.*

What professionals believe is of little value, unless demonstrated to the family. Professionals must, therefore, act respectfully; and must be seen to be respectful in their behaviour. For example, they should arrive on time, introduce themselves when appropriate and be courteous so that no superiority is implied. This refers to all aspects of behaviour, including non-verbal. We communicate powerfully by language, but also by our facial expression, direction of gaze, posture, body orientation, limb movements, tone of voice and so on. It is the combination of all these that tell us what another person feels and means.

Respect can be shown in many ways, but perhaps the most powerful is in *attending* to the family. Being prepared to listen and watch closely, rather than imposing and telling them what to do, immediately indicates that they are worthy of being taken seriously. It can be further shown by both verbal and non-verbal expressions of warmth. This means anything that can be done to indicate the professional's pleasure in seeing the family, whether by saying, 'It is good to see you again', or by smiling appropriately. Part of this process is the suspension of critical comments and avoidance of judgements about weaknesses or faults. At the same time it includes doing nothing to imply that the professional is better than the family, more able to cope or has taken over from them. Even a casual statement like 'I'll soon sort it out', may not only indicate the professional's intention and ability, but implies the families' inability and incompetence. Alternatively, showing pleasure at the successes achieved by the parents does signal respect. In fact, many of the following characteristics to be discussed will indicate this attitude fundamentally.

2. Genuineness

It is important for professionals to be genuine in all they do. The term is used to summarize a number of characteristics.

(i) *Sincerity and Honesty* Professionals should not pretend to be interested if they are not. In this case it might be better to refer the family to someone who is interested. False information should certainly never be given and in general, relevant information should not be withheld, though there is a dilemma here. Withholding may occasionally be justified on the grounds that the information may be damaging. In most cases where the professional can subsequently provide reasonable explanations for doing so, parents are satisfied and the relationship is not damaged. The dilemma is in judging what are reasonable reasons from the parental view. Certainly, if parents feel that the professional does not trust them to understand or use the information appropriately, then dissatisfaction is highly probable. It is for this reason that the counselling process is important as it provides professionals with information on the parent to guide such decisions.

(ii) *Enthusiasm* We assume that professionals should also work with enthusiasm. They should not behave in a detached, neutral manner, which may be interpreted as disinterest and have the effect of alienating the family. Behaving spontaneously, but not impulsively, is a manifestation of enthusiasm, willingness and lack of defensiveness. Spontaneity relies upon feeling confident, hence the importance of having a model of counselling.

(iii) *Openness* This implies an acceptance by professionals of themselves as they are and therefore not having to act a part for other people. Playing different roles for different people may be one basis for defensiveness occuring. It also implies that professionals should be able to accept new experiences and to change if necessary, as opposed to being rigid and fixed. This applies equally to professionals' perceptions of themselves and their constructions of the family. Openness in this way increases the ability to communicate what the parents are saying without imposing distortions on their meaning.

(iv) *Consistency and Trustworthiness* Under genuineness, we include the characteristics of consistency and trustworthiness. We stress consistency, because the family must get to know professionals well and be able to know what to expect from them. Of course, there may be a need to change with circumstances, but any resulting inconsistency should be noted by the professional. Being predictable in this way diminishes parental uncertainty. As parents gain confidence, they begin to trust and accept the professional's qualities. Trustworthiness is necessary so that the family can have faith in professionals' competence and can believe they will do what they say. The importance of this characteristic is particularly manifested in situations where the professional, in expressing one viewpoint, may be perceived as taking sides with a particular member of the family. Without trust, the professionals under such circumstances could be viewed as a threat, as working for one member against another. With trust, they may be seen as working with the family as a whole. Needless to say, taking sides should be avoided.

(v) Confidentiality   If the professional is to be trusted, the parents must believe that the information they provide will be confidential. It is important, therefore, to negotiate explicitly with them the extent to which this is true. This is part of the partnership contract. In fact, one cannot have a partnership based upon trust and respect, if one partner records and disseminates information without the agreement of the other.

3. Attending

Counselling is an active process, but paradoxically the central quality is listening. It helps establish the relationship by showing respect and genuineness and it enables the professional to gain an understanding of the parent's construct system and to begin to explore this with them. Talking so much that the conversation is dominated by the professional should be avoided. Lecturing to parents is also of little value, because, like moralizing, it imposes a point of view, as opposed to negotiating.

Attending means listening to what someone is saying and carefully considering the information. It also means listening to the ways they are saying it and watching what they are doing at the same time. As noted earlier, non-verbal aspects of communication are important: they serve to regulate (e.g. letting the other person know when it is their turn to speak); they say something about the words being used (e.g. endorsing the words); and they often indicate much about the general characteristics of the person and their emotional state at the time (e.g. anger, anxiety or happiness).

Non-verbal information can be grouped into five major categories. At any one time, all or some of these aspects of behaviour can provide significant information about the individual. There is, of course, no one-to-one relationship between a particular behaviour and what it signifies. It is up to the observer to interpret the significance, depending upon what the person is saying, the general situation in which it is being said and what is the constellation of all aspects of behaviour being shown.

(i) Paralinguistic information This refers not to the words used, but how they are delivered. It encompasses the accent of the person, the tone of voice, the speed of speech, the hesitations and errors. Anxiety, for example, may be indicated if the person speaks very quickly, stumbles over their words or uses 'um' or 'er' excessively. A long pause and hesitations may signal the occurrence of a subsequent embarrassing question or difficult issue.

(ii) Facial expression The face is a highly mobile pattern. It can vary in many ways and is very expressive. Smiles of different kinds can indicate information ranging from embarrassment to contentment. The colour of the face, from blushing to pallor, can also be included in this category.

(iii) Eye gaze The eyes are, of course, a part of the face, but they are such a powerful source of information that they warrant a category alone. The direction of the eyes indicates a great deal about the attention and feelings of the individual. Looking directly at the person indicates attention; it also shows willingness to interact and the desire to begin speaking. Looking away may indicate careful thought, anxiety or the desire to break off the conversation. Looking at, and even bending down to speak to a child, not only indicates concern for the child, but also communicates a great deal about the professional's characteristics that are important to the parents.

(iv) Movements Movements in general, though more commonly head, hand and arm movements, are sources of information. Gestures in themselves can be used instead of speech (e.g. shrugging the shoulders with the palms of the hands held outward indicates uncertainty) or to endorse or elaborate what is said (e.g. describing shapes). They can indicate anger or a range of other emotions such as boredom, frustration or anxiety. Touching is a movement that has powerful effects in our culture, where it is generally reserved for rather intimate situations.

(v) Body posture and orientation Considering the whole body, its posture can indicate a range of information from extreme relaxation and unconcern, to alertness and tension. Whether we are

lying down, sitting or standing will have different meanings. Leaning forward or slouching have different implications as well as the way we are facing. Sitting on the edge of a chair, for example, may be a clear indication of tenseness, stress, or excitement and enthusiasm.

If professionals are aware of such information and consider it carefully, they are in a better position to judge what people are really saying and how they are generally feeling. It may often be the consistency or inconsistency that is important to detect. For example, the parent who says, 'I love her dearly', yet does not look at the child may really be saying something like, 'I am trying to love her, but . . .'. The person who says, 'I'm fine' too quickly and then changes the subject may be indicating the reverse.

It is also important for the professional to consider the non-verbal information that they are providing for the parents. Firstly, by thinking about their own body, they may be more in touch with what is happening in the counselling situation. If, for example, they can feel themselves frowning, becoming tense or sitting more rigidly, it may indicate something important about the situation at that moment. Secondly, all that professionals say and do is interpreted by the parents. It indicates whether they are listening, whether they care, and what they value.

It is suggested, therefore, that a comfortable sitting position should be adopted. the professional and parents should be close, but not too close, and a desk or table should not be used as a protective barrier. They should sit facing each other, though perhaps at a slight angle. In general, the whole body should be orientated towards the parents, leaning forward slightly and certainly looking at them most of the time. Overall, the professional should appear relaxed and should not fidget excessively. Of course, there are no hard and fast rules, since we are all different and what is most comfortable for one person may not be for another. The general aim, however, is to set up a situation in which neither the professional nor the parents are distracted from the main purpose of the meeting. Professionals who are thinking about how uncomfortable they feel are unlikely to be attending to the parents in the ways we have described. Certainly parents are sensitive to these behaviours, if in appropriate. For example, parents may comment upon the paediatrician's tendency to avoid looking at them, or the teacher's nervousness being manifested by looking at and shuffling papers when asked a question.

It is important to be aware of an array of factors that might distract from effective attention. They may include tiredness, preoccupation with other matters such as other work problems, personal health and anxieties about the ability to help the family. Strong feelings, even negative ones, about the family may interfere, and an overconcern with one's professional role may have the same effects. Whatever it is that is distracting from active attention must be overcome, and can be by an extra effort to concentrate upon the talker and a careful analysis of what one is thinking and feeling and why. This is another example of why professionals should be in touch with themselves and understand themselves as well as possible.

4. Getting Parents to Talk

Parents will usually talk openly and willingly, because someone is at last listening to them. However, the professional will at times want to guide the direction of the conversation, if the parent is particularly garrulous, or to facilitate conversation, if the parents are reluctant to begin or get stuck. There are many ways of doing this, and the most common are:

(i) *Questions* Open-ended questions are those that cannot be answered with a single, simple, fixed reply; for example, 'How have things been going?' or 'How have you been getting on with . . .?' Closed questions, on the other hand, ask for specific information, (e.g. 'How many children have you?'). Although closed questions may be used, it is preferable to use open questions as a first resort to allow parents to reply in the way that suits them. They are therefore in control of what information is provided. Such questions are less directive and formal than closed questions and may be used to initiate or extend the conversation. They are useful in getting the parents to explore topics in their own ways, which could not be done by a barrage of formal closed questions that are more closely related to the professional's interpretations or intentions than the parents'. The use of the word 'problem' even in an open-ended question (e.g. 'Would you like to discuss your problems') is to be avoided when first meeting parents. This is because it makes the assumption that they have problems, and it signifies that the professional's interest is only in the parent's weaknesses. Similarly, the need to choose words very carefully so as not to make unwarranted assumptions is illustrated by the open-question 'What can I do for you?' which wrongly implies that the responsibility for action is with the professional and not the parents. If there remain specific pieces of information to be

elicited once more open questions have been asked, these can
of course be sought by closed questions.

(ii) Statements   When the conversation has been initiated, a gentler
way of allowing the parents to explore their situation is the use
of statements and not questions. For example, 'That sounds like
a difficult situation' may not only show that the professional is
attending and understands, but may also prompt the parents to
continue talking in more depth. Depending upon the content of
the statement, they might also be guided to address specific issues
in this way. For example, by saying something like 'You must
have been annoyed' in response to a description of a child's
naughtiness may gently direct the parent to talk about their own
feelings as opposed to the child's behaviour.

(iii) Other prompts   Another way of gently prompting the parents
to continue is to nod the head or say something like 'yes' or 'mm-
mm'. In fact, if you watch listeners in a conversation, they will
be doing just this in order to signal on-going attention. An alternative, and this is somewhat more directive, is to ask a question
by repeating the parent's words with a questioning inflection.
For example, if a mother said, 'She came home in a foul mood',
the professional's response of 'In a foul mood?' would be likely
to prompt the mother to elaborate what she meant.

(iv) Silence   Brief periods of silence sensitively used will often
allow the parent to say something further. This might be useful
in allowing them a short pause in order to think or to feel an
emotion. Such pauses in themselves may show that the professional understands and respects their feelings. Judicious use of
pauses may prompt parents to discuss deeper feelings or worries.
Again they should not be overused, because they may become
unsettling and appear manipulative.

(v) Commands   We have implied in this list a dimension of the
degree of directiveness asserted by the professional. Although
in general the family should be allowed to direct the explorations
of their situation, there are times when their attention must either
subtly, or overtly be directed. The most directive of the behaviours
so far mentioned is probably the use of closed questions, but direct
commands can be used; for example, 'Go on' or 'Tell me more
about that'. There may be a degree of urgency in this way that
would not occur in another way of saying the same thing, as
in the use of questions such as 'Can you tell me more?'

5. Empathy

What we mean by empathy is the attempt to understand the way the parents construe their world. This involves trying to put onself 'in the shoes' of the parents in order to see what sense they make of their situation. This is a process fraught with difficulties, because no-one can ever totally understand another person in all respects, and because we always tend to construe other people on the basis of our own ways of perceiving. This is the reason why openness was so strongly stressed earlier; if we have an open mind, then we can be receptive to the ways others construe events. The aim is to try to enunciate the parent's current framework together.

As we noted earlier, it is vital not just to be empathic, but also to communicate this to the family. Here again is the importance of not distorting information. There is a need not only for an understanding of the person, but also to be able to express the understanding precisely and clearly, and, of course, accurately. If this is done successfully it will have at least two effects. One is that the rapport between the professional and the parents will be aided, the parents are likely to be more trusting, more open in what they say and more respectful in that they will feel that the professional not only makes the effort, but also understands them. Secondly, empathic statements will help the parents to explore and clarify their understanding of their present situation.

At a basic level, therefore, professionals must show the parents that they understand by reflecting their meaning back to them. This is not indicated by statements such as 'I understand' or 'I know how you feel'. Rather it is demonstrated by making statements that succinctly express the parents' meaning. For example, 'You feel you are not as capable as you should be' was an empathic response to a mother saying 'She keeps crying, no matter what I do, whereas other people seem to be able to distract her'.

Of course, whatever parents say, they are expressing many different meanings at the same time and consequently there are a range of remarks that could be made that would be seen by parents as understanding. It is like attempting to hit a target with an arrow. Many arrows may be accurate, but only a few hit the bull. The skill is to capture succinctly the true essence of the parents' meaning (to hit the bullseye). That this has been achieved may be indicated by the liveliness of the parent's subsequent response. For example, a mother described visits to various professionals to seek advice about her son's failure to read. She finished by saying that they all thought she was troublesome and neurotic. The professional replied, 'But you were prepared to suffer this indignity, because your son is more important than your pride', to which the mother replied immediately, 'That's right. Why haven't all these others understood?'

As in all interpersonal skills, it is important not to overuse empathic statements. They may be used when the parents are talking about something significant. They should be used responsibly and not in a way that intrudes or interrupts. The professional should not simply parrot the parent's remarks, nor pretend to understand or guess when they are unclear. In this case, it is better to ask them to clarify what they are saying. Professionals should be reasonably certain that they will be accurate, and should not be long-winded, thereby taking over from the parents. Within reason, the tone, manner and language used should reflect that of the parent. Something said slowly and seriously, for example, should not usually produce a gleeful reply.

6. Challenging Skills

The characteristics which have been discussed are largely concerned with establishing an effective relationship with the family and creating the kind of atmosphere in which a partnership can exist. They have also been the kinds of skills necessary to get the parents to explore their situation and to clarify their understanding of it, as well as to enable the professional to understand. We have perhaps implied that the partnership is a one-way affair with information and direction being provided by the parents. This may be true to an extent at first. However, counselling is a process of negotiation between partners. The parents may not already have the best understanding of themselves, their child and their general situation in terms of enabling them to adjust most effectively.

The task of counselling is not just to accept the parents' construct system, but to help them change it. To do this the professional should be skilled in ways of placing demands upon the parents; *challenging* them to change. Deciding when the time is right to do this is not easy, but the function is to:

(1) enable them to participate in the partnership;
(2) help them clarify further their own constructs;
(3) help them develop new perspectives or constructs.

There are a number of ways of doing this, but in general serious challenges should only occur once an adequate relationship has been established, when the professional has been accepted as trustworthy, competent and empathic. Prior to this challenges may be much too threatening. Nevertheless, with care, alternative hypotheses, which have not previously been considered by the parents and are in this respect challenging, may be offered early in the relationship, and may indicate the professional's competence and usefulness. Even later, when an appropriate relationship has developed, any challenge must to some extent be threatening so as to initiate change. Therefore, they should be given in a way that invites change, rather than commands it. Different ways of doing this will be described in turn.

(i) *'What we have talked about so far is . . .'* The professional briefly summarizes what has happened in the previous meeting or in the present session up to that point. It may be useful as a way of orientating the parents at the beginning of a session or focusing the meeting when it has begun to ramble or the parents have got stuck. The skill serves to show that the professional is interested, is competent and understands, and may invite future discussion and exploration of particular areas. It may, however, be challenging in that the counsellor puts together a set of ideas from the past that may present a wider framework that has not previously been seen by the parents.

(ii) *'That is not quite right . . .'* Providing new information or alternative explanations, correcting misinformation or helping the parents to obtain information for themselves can also be regarded as challenging in the sense that they have to change so as to incorporate this new material. Their understanding of their situation will change if they are given such information. Telling parents, for example, about the nature of their child's learning difficulties and the likely outcome *invites* them to accept the information and to incorporate it in their construct system.

(iii) *'Your wife's acceptance of the problem makes you feel guilty'.* This is advanced empathy and relates closely to what we said earlier about empathy (i.e. communicating an understanding of what the parents feel). However, it goes a step further. It challenges the parents, because it reflects back to them, not what they have said directly, but what they have only implied, or mean, but may have hidden. It holds up to the parents an implication of their understanding of the situation and in doing so faces them with a new perspective. It might involve expressing clearly what they have said vaguely, drawing conclusions that they have not drawn or connecting issues that have been discussed as separate. For example, in response to a mother's long monologue about arguments with her husband which then moved unsolicited into worries about the correctness of her actions in relation to her child, the professional said:

> You talked of your husband and then seemed to connect this with
> your sudden fears that you are a poor mother. I just wonder

whether you are beginning to think of yourself as generally not
very competent, because your husband seems to be criticising all
the time.

This sets up an idea to be explored in discussion, even if it is
subsequently rejected.

(iv) 'It seems to me that you are not being realistic'. This may be called
confrontation. Whereas advanced empathy takes what the parent
says and attempts to clarify their own meaning, confrontation
involves looking at the parents from outside, and making judgements about them. An alternative view is given of the parent's
behaviour, and since this may be seen as criticism, and therefore
embarrassing and threatening, it is perhaps potentially the most
difficult to use. Confrontations try to point out or challenge dis-
crepancies that occur either in the interview session or outside.
For example, having listened to a father constantly discussing only
his child's academic qualities, the teacher said 'I've noticed that
you only talk about your son's school performance. I wonder
whether you acknowledge the importance of other personal qualities.' Similarly, if the parents are seen to be distorting reality in
some way or expressing self-defeating constructs, then it may be
appropriate to confront them with what they are doing, for
example, 'You are assuming that your child's learning difficulties
make him a useless person all round'. It may also be necessary
at times to confront the parents in relation to their behaviour towards the professional, if they act in ways that make the sessions
unproductive in some way. This is very much related to the next
general skill.

(v) 'We don't seem to be getting anywhere ...'   In everyday interactions we tend to talk about any subject apart from the immediate
behaviour of the talker and listener. Because it may be embarrassing, it is very difficult to comment on the behaviour of the person
to whom we are talking even if their actions are rather disconcert-
ing and strange. In counselling, however, it is important to be
able to make such comments, because it may be the interpersonal
behaviour of the parents that is causing or, at least, related to
their difficulties. We will call this skill, immediacy. For example,
being able to say that the session has become directionless or
that it is very tense, may allow exploration of these points and
therefore provide direction or an understanding of the tension.
The following comment by a speech therapist, 'When you replied
to my question, I thought I had upset you, because you seemed
very angry and a little aggressive towards me' led to a very useful
discussion of a problem the parents were having with the head

of a special school and the father's feelings that the therapist was probably also 'on the side of the authorities'.

(vi) 'I feel like that when my own children won't do what I tell them.' Self-disclosure is a useful way of establishing empathy and reducing the expert barrier, particularly in the early stages of the relationship. Although it should never be overused or become a burden to parents, remarks made by professionals about themselves may be valuable. An honest remark such as 'I feel a failure when my own child does badly at school' may not only help parents to put their own behaviour and experience into perspective, but may also indicate the honesty and vulnerability of the professional. However, if overused, it can become a woeful interchange.

The use of challenge is one of the most difficult skills in counselling, because of the threat it implies to the parent and the potential damage to the relationship. Paradoxically, it is the first method adopted by many professionals, which may explain poor rates of compliance and high dissatisfaction with professional advice. Where possible it is preferable to challenge the parents subtly, so that they feel that they have understood the issue by their own efforts. Serious confrontation, therefore, is a last resort, since this is where professionals are expressing their own understandings and their own expertise. Whether or not the professional knows what actions the parents have to take from the beginning, the parents should be helped to reach conclusions by their own efforts. Particular techniques should be employed only if they serve a purpose in relation to the goals of the interview and if the parent–professional relationship is sufficiently robust. If the relationship is mutually respectful then confrontations are more likely to be taken seriously; if not, they may simply be threatening and dismissed as malicious or stupid.

In most parent–professional interactions the parents are likely to be particularly sensitive and vulnerable. This heightened sensitivity demands that, whatever the challenge, it should be made without accusation. It should not be done in a commanding way, yet it should not be so meek and hesitant that it is missed or dismissed. The challenge should also be concrete and specific, not an abstract generalization. The parent ought not to feel trapped by the challenge, but able to move. This may be facilitated by emphasizing their strengths, not weaknesses, and by offering constructive suggestions for them to consider.

The Process of Counselling

The above skills are valuable in any situation with parents, even in a one-off ten-minute meeting. The process below may occur to an extent even here. However, it is more likely if there are a number of regular meetings prearranged at mutually convenient intervals. Looking at the sessions as a whole, it is an ever changing process, in which the characteristics discussed above may be required constantly or employed more selectively at different times. It is not possible to say what will occur in counselling at what time precisely, nor how long it will take. So much depends upon the characteristics of the professional, the family, the issues addressed, their relationship, and the techniques used. It may be, for example, that a strong and effective relationship is established in minutes, or takes several weeks. Nevertheless, it is useful to try to anticipate possible phases of the process and to discuss the requirements in counselling skills in each. The process is represented diagrammatically in Figure 6.

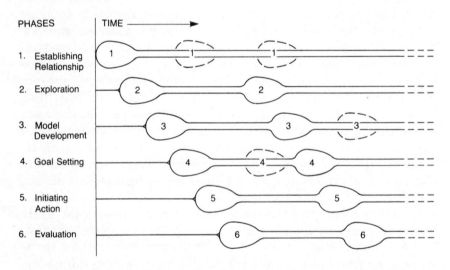

Figure 6   The Process of Counselling: Diagrammatic Representation of Phases: The bubbles represent the focus of counselling at a particular time with dotted bubbles illustrating possible irregularities, and overlaps. The parallel lines represent the simultaneous and ongoing nature of each of the activities.

We will look at the process chronologically, but it is important to note that in any session there may be oscillation between phases. The model, therefore, is for guidance not adherence. For example, at the first meeting, the professional may be able to offer advice which immediately allows the parent to take positive action. The health visitor may make a suggestion to overcome a feeding difficulty; the speech therapist may ask parents to record words used by the child in preparation for the next meeting. Such suggestions must be very carefully considered, as failure could seriously affect the relationship. Success demonstrates both parent and professional competence and lays a firm foundation for the partnership. Overall, however, there is a very great need to plan what is intended in each session, whether this is to explore the parents' views and feelings further or to devise a specific programme of exercise, or decide upon an aspect of diet. Each meeting should be approached with a specific aim, based upon notes made after the last session, and looked at carefully before the next. At the end of the session the professional can then evaluate to what extent the aims were met in the session and make a note of it when briefly recording what happened.

1. Establishing the Relationship

This is the first stage and is important both because it meets some of the aims of counselling in itself (e.g. supporting the family) and because it is a pre-requisite for all subsequent effects and actions. As we have said, it does not simply involve one or two sentences to relax the parents; it is a much deeper process. It means motivating the family to work with the professional by getting them involved in the process, so that at least initially they are willing to discuss themselves and problem situations openly. They must be able to do this in order to explore their situation thoroughly. This is facilitated by the fundamental qualities of actively attending, respecting and being genuine and empathic from the beginning of the first session. The venue should be comfortable, informal and private, and meeting the parents in their home is advantageous.

Part of establishing a relationship is the process of coming to a joint agreement about the nature of counselling. This involves professionals in (1) describing their roles; (2) discussing general concepts such as working in partnership and even describing the process as outlined here; and (3) negotiating aims that are acceptable to the parents. Clearly what is decided at this point is only an initial 'contract' and is open to renegotiation, clarification and change by both partners.

This initial step is often neglected. Professionals frequently neither introduce themselves nor describe their role, let alone negotiate it. They assume, mistakenly, that the parents already understand all this, as though the parent and the professional shared the same constructs prior to the onset of counselling. The essential purpose of the agreement is to allow the professional and parents to know what to expect of each other. This means to be able to construe each other and therefore anticipate what each is likely to do and how to behave in return. This is particularly important as the parents' perceived satisfaction with counselling will be closely dependent upon their expectations of it.

2. Exploration

The next phase is the exploration of the families' situation. As can be seen in Figure 6, this begins in and overlaps with the first phase, though it was not initially the primary focus. It is not a diagnostic process in the sense of imposing a model upon the family situation, but an exploration of how the parents construe their situation, themselves, their children and their resources, needs and goals. In the spirit of a partnership, it is not just a process of giving information to the professional who can then understand and make decisions. It is true that the professional must try to understand how parents construe their situation, but the main intention is that the parents *clarify for themselves* their ways of construing. For example, why do they think the child is not walking, is waking at night or is unhappy and irritable. In a behavioural approach this would be called functional analysis and would involve the use of such things as systematic observations and checklists, which are most useful and perfectly valid. However, what is important is that one explores all possible explanations by all the means that are available and not just those that are based upon one set of notions and associated techniques.

Exploration, then has purpose for both the professional and the parent in that they develop a better understanding of their situation. The process is set in motion with such open-ended questions, discussed earlier, as 'Would you like to tell me what has happened?' The general objective is to facilitate discussion; to allow the parents to talk about their own situation in a tolerant and permissive setting. All the skills and counselling characteristics described earlier, apart from challenging, may play a large part here, particularly those of motivating parents to talk and guiding the discussion.

The outcome to be expected is that the parents become clearly aware of the situation as they see it. Using observation in a systematic or unsystematic way they might notice a regular pattern in the circumstances surrounding a child's tantrums or aggression. They may have noticed the consistency, but have explained in one way when there may be several possible explanations. Only when they have explored are they in a position to evaluate the adequacy of their understanding and be able to set clear goals for what they must do. If, for example, in exploring their situation, parents realize that they love each other, wish to remain together and that their arguments are damaging their child, then their model may be adequate for deciding their goals (e.g. to show each other affection). The process of clarification may often serve to show the parents that what the paediatrician or the teacher had told them about their child was not clear. In this case the first goal would be to request further explanation from these professionals, so that the parents may be in a position to construe their situation more adequately.

3. Model Development

As in the last example where the process of exploration has indicated that their model or ways of construing their situation is inadequate, the next major phase of counselling involves working with the family so that effective models may be developed. It may be that the parents construe themselves in self-defeating ways by seeing themselves as, for example, 'unable to cope'. It may be that they have drawn defeatist conclusions (e.g. 'They (the professionals) never listen to me. I don't know anything. I can't help my child'). The parents may simply not know what confronts them. For example, they may not know the meaning of dyslexia or cerebral palsy, or what the teacher means when referring to a slow reader. In such cases, their model is obviously inadequate in that they do not have necessary information. Again, they may have inaccurate constructs (e.g. 'the mentally handicapped can't learn anything' or 'parents who have handicapped children are likely to get divorced').

Whatever the inadequacies of the construct system, the aim in this phase is to facilitate the development of a more useful system, which enables them to anticipate what to do. The parents need to change. In some cases this may occur easily, but in others it may be extremely difficult. For example, a mother of a five year old girl with severe cerebral palsy saw her child as 'totally normal' intellectually on the basis of her conversational ability which was more than adequate in the home. As a result she was unable to accept that there was a considerable delay in both her expressive and receptive language and that her learning was hampered by behavioural problems at school. She believed none of the professionals who directly confronted her with the 'truth', much to their extreme consternation and annoyance. Only when an effective relationship of the type we have discussed was established was mother able to begin to change. Only then could challenging skills be brought to bear, to provide a wider perspective, a different model or alternative explanations from which to select. This was backed up by including the mother in all the assessments that were made of the child's behaviour and in the designing of an appropriate remedial programme which included the use of reinforcement.

Individuals do not change easily; we are all somewhat conservative in this respect. If there are pressures on us to change, this creates a conflict between the way we have construed our situation and the new suggested ways of construing it. For example, if a parent has construed her child as functioning adequately at school, the information that remedial help is necessary produces just this sort of conflict. In one example, a nine year old came home from school and told his parents that he was a slow learner and that the teacher had said that he had to have special help in reading. Such news is hurtful enough, if given caringly and carefully, but to do it without thought, as in this case, distressed the child and shocked the parents. They had had no warning of this conflicting information, and as a result they were angry with the school, and the relationship between them and the teacher was damaged. This, however, gave them a partial way out of the conflict, because they could blame the situation upon the incompetence of the teacher, rather than explore the truth of the child's difficulties.

We all attempt to reduce conflict and we can do so in a number of ways. In the counselling situation, parents could simply believe what the professional says and change their ways of construing. Alternatively, they could discredit the professional (e.g. 'He doesn't understand'); look for support elsewhere (e.g. 'The health visitor said quite the reverse') or to try to change the professional's viewpoint. To increase the probability of the parents changing, it is important to reduce the possibility of the alternatives. If professionals are seen as attractive, trustworthy and competent then their views are more likely to be taken seriously and less easily dismissed.

4. Goal Setting

Once an adequate, realistic model is available to the parents, they are then in a position to make decisions about what directions they can pursue and what aims they can set. This, in turn, is the basis for exploring possible strategies for achieving these aims. The next phase in the counselling process is, therefore, to enable the parents to formulate their goals.

For example, with the parents of a child of average intelligence with severe reading difficulties, the teacher was able to help them to change their model of their child as 'not much good at school and we will just have to accept it', to one of 'He is not generally incompetent in all school work, but he has a specific difficulty in learning to read which is making other learning difficult and destroying his confidence'. On this basis the parents aimed to 'do everything possible to improve his reading', as opposed to the aim from the original model, which had been 'to make him happy and stop him being bored'. Although the latter was perfectly acceptable, their resulting actions would have been totally different.

The aim in the above example of encouraging reading was useful in giving general direction and long term goals, but it was not adequate for deciding specifically what the parents should do; it was too general. This point is stressed because it is very important that the parents be helped to decide upon goals that are specific, concrete, clear, realistic, appropriate, verifiable and set within reasonable time limits. 'To be able to understand commonly displayed public signs' is specific, clear and concrete, but it is also verifiable in that its achievement or otherwise can be assessed. This is precisely what would be expected to result from an analysis using a behavioural approach. However, whether it is appropriate or realistic depends upon the child. It is appropriate if it can form the basis of what actions should be taken by the parents and would lead to a significant step or advance. It would be realistic within a specified period.

It is, however, better to underestimate somewhat, because if the parents should experience early failure in achieving their goals, they are likely to lose confidence in themselves and the professional. Success, on the onther hand, will motivate them further. When a goal is found to be too low, it may nevertheless form one of a number of subgoals in the path towards more effective functioning.

We have included setting of reasonable time limits in the list because of the importance of succeeding and knowing when one may expect to have succeeded. 'To be able to read common public signs, within three months' prevents the parents from experiencing failure after only a week, and yet is also provides time for them to evaluate their efforts within the period, so that new goals may be set, if necessary.

5. Initiating Action

Given that they have set appropriate goals then the next step in counselling is to help the parents to decide methods of achieving them. Having identified the sources of stress and decided the aims, the question is to decide strategies to achieve the aims and reduce the stress. There are, of course, all sorts of alternative strategies that may be adopted, and it is the professional's task to enable parents to discover all the possibilities and to select those considered appropriate and available. A common first choice must be to decide whether to:

(a) Work with the child themselves.
(b) Obtain professional help.
(c) Do both.

In the case of (a) or (c), the professional will need to either train the parents directly or introduce them to another source of help. In the case of (b) they may need to prepare parents to interact with other professionals by, for example, sharing counselling skills with them or giving them training in assertiveness, so that they can communicate better and even challenge other professionals.

The professional's task is to help parents discover in detail all the possibilities. They are then in a position to make the most informed decisions about what to do. The decisions can be made on the basis of the cost-effectiveness of each of the alternatives. The parents may be helped to decide what the alternatives require in terms of resources (money, time, effort, skills, etc.); what resources are available to them; and what would be the anticipated success following the outlays made. Should they spend two hours a day doing physiotherapy exercises to enable the infant to sit up unsupported? Do they have this amount of time and even if they do, is the goal likely to be achieved? Whatever the decision, the action to be taken should, like goals, be specified clearly and concretely and should be realistic, appropriate and related to the aims to be achieved. It is of relatively little value for the health visitor to help the parents decide to stimulate the child. Rather they should know what sort of stimulation is to be provided, when, where and how. In deciding what actions to take, consideration has to be given to the skills and abilities that will be required, and again, one has to consider the cost-effectiveness of alternative strategies.

6. Evaluation

While parents are carrying out their decided strategies, the role of the professional is still that of supporter. This may involve encouragement, advice, discussion and where necessary help for the parents to revise their goals and methods in the light of their experience. Throughout, therefore, there is the need for constant monitoring, but certainly the process of evaluation is essential once a given strategy has been carried out.

It is a most important phase of the counselling process that the parents are helped to look closely at what they have done and to evaluate whether the goals they set have been accomplished by the strategies adopted. Whether the goals have been achieved completely, partially or not at all, the process is the same to some extent. If completely successful, then the next step is to decide upon the next goal to be achieved and the method of doing so.

It might be that the problem has been resolved by achieving the goals set and therefore the professional and family have to re-evaluate their partnership. It may well be the case that the counselling has become redundant and should, therefore, end. If the goals have not been achieved, or only partly achieved, then the professionals must help the family to decide the reasons. As a result, the methods may be changed and/or revised goals set. On the other hand, it might be that the parent's general view of the situation has changed as a consequence of what they have done. For example, one family attempted to tackle the problem of the child not going to sleep until very late each evening. Although their goal was not achieved (i.e. 'going to sleep within half an hour of being put to bed') they did improve the situation in that the child played quietly in his bedroom and did not disturb the parents. As a result of their experience, they decided that they were no longer concerned about the sleeplessness and, therefore, need not pursue the goal.

As in the phase of the development of the parent's model, so in the evaluation stage the skills of attending, active listening, directing parents' explorations and challenging them, as well as the fundamental attributes of respecting, empathy and genuineness remain vital to the success of the whole counselling enterprise.

That there is an evaluation stage implies that the agreed plans of action are not guaranteed to achieve success. They are a means to test the hypotheses derived from the model development phase. This final stage can, therefore, serve to remind both parents and professional that they are in the process of experimenting or acting scientifically. If this philosophy is accepted then parents and professionals may be more able to deal with lack of success and its consequent reduction of motivation.

Concluding Comments

The process of counselling most frequently involves the professional in an attempt to help parents change. The focus will often, though not always, be upon enabling parents to change the behaviour of their children. Whether it is the professional attempting to change the parents or the parents attempting to change their child, or even the professional directly attempting to change the child, the process is the same as that above. In all cases underlying this process are a number of basic principles which will be described below. At the heart of all the principles are respect and negotiation, the foundations of partnership endorsed throughout the book. Being a child, even with special needs, does not invalidate our arguments about respecting those with whom we are working, as well as listening to them, being genuine and so on.

1. Working from the Known to the Unknown: Just as the professional listens closely to parents, attempts to understand them and uses this as a basis for helping them, so parents must begin their efforts from a through knowledge of the child, in terms of his/her skills, abilities and constructs.
2. Working at the Pace of the Person Being Changed: In counselling the professional must proceed at a speed negotiated with the parents. Moving too quickly or procrastinating when they wish to proceed are equally likely to produce alienation. Similarly, expecting the child to change when not ready, or moving too slowly, will only produce failure or loss of interest. To some extent, therefore, control of the process must be in the hands of the person being changed.
3. Ensuring the Relevance of Change: Just as parents are less likely to change if the professional makes demands on them to change in ways that are construed as unacceptable and irrelevant, so the relevance of changes requested from children should be considered, and negotiated wherever possible.
4. Setting Explicit Goals: In working with parents or with children, explicit goals should be set and wherever possible negotiated, or at the very least demonstrated. This is not only so that all concerned know what they are attempting, but also so that they know whether it has been achieved.

5. Maximizing Success: In attempting to change both parents and children, realistic goals should be set in order to maximize success. In both cases failure to do this will lead to loss of confidence and reduced effort. A crucial factor to consider, therefore, is the amount of change requested in any one step.

6. Emphasizing Self-Responsibility: Throughout the book we have returned at various points to respecting those with whom we work and emphasizing their self-responsibility. This is equally true whether it is the professional changing the parents or the parents changing their child. The intention is to facilitate in both cases feelings of self-confidence, self-esteem and self-efficacy.

Practical Exercise

A.   All the skills described in this chapter must be practised, and this can be done by using them in everyday life. For example, you can try to listen closely and attend carefully to what your friends are saying. Try to make statements that are empathic or try to guide conversations by prompting and facilitating in the ways we have suggested.

Since, in the acquisition of a skill, it is essential to have feedback on performance, it is also necessary to practise in co-operation with other people. We would suggest, therefore, that you carry out this exercise in the company of at least one other person, such as a colleague. It is perhaps better, however, if there are three people so that you can interact, with one taking the role of parent, another the role of counsellor and the third as an observer who can then comment upon what was observed.

1. Decide who is to be the counsellor, parent and observer and set up an acted counselling session lasting no more than five minutes. It is often useful for the 'parent' to take a disturbing or annoying experience from their own life to be discussed in the counselling.

2. Concentrate upon one of the skills that we have described at a time. You may well use others simultaneously, but plan to focus upon one and do it as well as you can. Attend closely, or try to be empathic (at a basic or advanced level) or challenge the person in the ways discussed. Attempt to be genuine or respectful, and so on. If necessary, the 'parent' may be asked to act in specific ways (e.g. showing

anger, reticence, confusion) or adopting a specified framework to allow the 'counsellor' to practise particular
strategies.

3. At the end of the role-play, discuss the performance. How
   did you feel the 'counsellor' did? How did the 'parent' feel?
   What are the observer's comments? Consider what you did
   wrong and how you could improve.

4. A further way of providing feedback is to audiotape record
   the session and then listen to and discuss it. Videorecording
   will, of course, add an extra dimension if the equipment
   is available.

5. The next step may be to try again to improve what was
   wrong last time and to repeat the feedback discussion.
   Before doing so, it might be valuable to rehearse several
   times a particular type of response (e.g. the tone of voice
   when having to challenge something assertively).

6. Next, change places, so that the 'parent' becomes the
   observer or 'counsellor' and so on until everyone has played
   each part. Each time repeat the evaluation feedback and
   rehearsal if necessary.

7. Then take another specific skill or difficult situation and
   focus the practice on it. Again take turns trying it.

This should occur over several meetings. At first you may feel
embarrassed and worried about criticism, but you should quickly
get used to the situation. It is important, however, to be positive
and constructive in evaluating the performance of someone else.

B.   This is a heavily edited transcript taken from a much longer
interview. Read it through carefully until you get the feel of what
is going on. Then:

1. Take each of the counsellor's remarks in turn and try to
   judge into which of the following categories it fits – prompting the parents to talk, open or closed question, empathy,
   summarizing, providing new information, advanced
   empathy, confrontation, a comment on the counselling relationship (immediacy) or self-disclosure. A given statement
   may fit into several categories.

2. Judge whether each of the counsellor's remarks are accurate
   or appropriate. Consider whether you would have said the
   same.

Mother: I get really upset when I watch the teacher work-
             ing with him so well.

Counsellor:	Mm-hm
Mother:	He really tries and enjoys it.
Counsellor:	How does it upset you?
Mother:	Well! He won't do anything for me. He just mucks about.
Counsellor:	I suppose that makes you feel useless.
Mother:	Yes. All the time.
Counsellor:	I often feel like that with my son. Perhaps it's a problem of being a parent.
Mother:	You mean parents shouldn't teach their children.
Counsellor:	No. But perhaps the relationship makes it more difficult.
Mother:	It's alright when the rest of the family are around. He's happy then and I feel better.
Counsellor:	You seem to be saying that you can't teach him yourself, but you can provide other things when the family are around.
Mother:	Well! He's happy when we're all together. But, somehow I feel we should do more than that.
Counsellor:	You think happniness isn't important.
Mother:	It's not quite that. I just want him to be able to do all the things he can't. Maybe I'm also being selfish and don't want all the fuss.
Counsellor:	And that makes you all the more worried that you're not constantly trying.
Mother:	It's a vicious circle. I try, and he wants to do something else. I get angry, which upsets him, so I do something nice and I think he knows how to make me stop teaching him.
Counsellor:	It looks to me like he's controlling you very well. Perhaps he isn't as slow as you think. It also looks like you're contradicting yourself by trying to make him happy, yet thinking that happiness isn't important.

CHAPTER 7

How Parents Participate

In this chapter a number of current approaches and specific projects concerned with parent participation will be described. They will be used to illustrate the application of the frameworks, principles and skills noted in previous chapters in relation to the major needs of providing information, emotional and practical support and guidance and training. This will include how such principles are equally as relevant to group situations as to one-to-one relationships. The involvement of parents in activities such as providing transport, fund raising, parent–professional associations and assisting in classrooms will not be considered. They are often reactions to the needs of professionals, rather than intended to meet parental needs and create a partnership. Eric Midwinter (1977) in his book, *Education For Sale*, characterized the extreme of this clearly when he said: 'A mute coolie with a full wallet would seem to be some head's image of the perfect parent'. It is recognized, however, that these reactions to the needs of professionals can be mutually beneficial and provide important services and points of contact for the development of parent–professional collaboration. Nor will we consider the provision of basic services such as special aids, health care, financial assistance and housing problems. These are important and family functioning can often be helped far more by the provision of a washing machine or increased mobility than attending a therapeutic group or receiving sympathetic support. Indeed, many studies conclude that meeting utilitarian needs is the first priority for families.

Although it is beyond the scope of this book, mention has to be made of the rapidly developing area of family therapy (Walrond–Skinner, 1981). Many of the principles that have been discussed in the earlier chapters are relevant to this approach. The term, family therapy, refers to a diverse range of theoretical frameworks and techniques generally used by specialists in child psychiatry, including clinical psychologists, social workers, psychotherapists and psychiatrists. The approach is firmly based upon the principle that children do not have behavioural disturbance in isolation from the family. Therefore, typically the whole family is interviewed together in order to explore openly the problem of the referred child in relation to all members of the family. For example, it may be that the problem relates more closely to a non-referred family member or to the structure and functioning of the family as a whole. Through a series of meetings an attempt is made to define the problem and devise therapeutic strategies. Most professionals dealing with parents will need to be aware of the availability of family therapy for referral if necessary, but will not need the rather specialized frameworks or skills of this area.

We will begin by discussing one of the more common approaches to parent participation which is the use of parent groups, because it exemplifies many of the basic principles.

Parent Groups

Because professional resources are scarce, working in groups can be more economical than working with individual families, providing it meets their needs. A second advantage is that parents can help each other. In consequence, there has been a rapid expansion of parent group approaches over the last twenty or so years (Seligman, 1982). The early work tended to be an extension of clinical psychiatric practice aimed principally at helping parents to adjust to the child's handicap and focused on attitudes, feelings and emotional problems. To some extent this reflected the pathological orientation discussed earlier, in which parents of children with a severe handicap were automatically assumed to have emotional problems. Many groups were made up of parents referred by clinical agencies and were run by psychiatrists and social workers.

Like all parent groups, these therapeutic groups aimed at improving parental effectiveness. It was argued that unless the parents had emotionally adjusted and come to terms with themselves and the child's handicap, their relationship with the child would be impaired. These approaches also recognized that this adjustment required emotional support which was more likely to be gained from group than individual methods. Groups can reduce feelings of isolation and provide a wider support network, and also parents are often more ready to accept comments from other parents than from professionals and gain insights from shared experiences.

Since the emphasis in such groups is 'client-centred' and the aims are to promote awareness and understanding of feelings and reduced anxiety, they are usually informal, with open-ended discussions. Reflective counselling techniques (Chapter 6) are used to encourage the expression of feelings, to identify problems of greatest concern and to devise strategies for coping with them. The parents set the agenda and largely control the direction, pace and frequency of the meetings. Some approaches have also included the goal of changing parental attitudes to child rearing. Whilst the emphasis has been on small group discussions, other methods such as lectures, question and answer sessions with a panel, films, written material and role play have been included.

With the emergence of behavioural theories and the shift toward sharing skills with parents, more formal groups, often called 'workshops', were set up. The main focus was that of providing advice, guidance and training in order to participate directly in the child's treatment or education. Some were also a reaction against the 'reflective' approach, which often appeared to assume that all parents of handicapped children required counselling for unresolved emotional difficulties. Instead it was argued that the parents' main need was to learn management and teaching skills and that the more capable parents were in controlling behaviour problems and developing skills in the child, the less likely they are to experience stress and emotional upset. Most behavioural workshops, however, focused on the child's as opposed to the parents' needs, the main rationale being:

(i) that parents could provide more one-to-one teaching considered necessary for children with difficulties;

(ii) parents could consolidate at home and elsewhere the learning taken place in the classroom and therefore help generalize and maintain the learning;

(iii) in the case of behavioural problems, it was argued that these often related directly to parental behaviour and that it was these that needed to be changed.

Workshops generally, therefore, have in common the aim of developing in parents educational and management skills which are applied to their child's current behavioural problem or learning difficulties. Most also aim to increase parent confidence, by sharing experiences with other parents, confirming their competence and developing new skills. Consequently, emphasis is given to tackling child behaviours which are both relevant and modifiable within the time span of the workshop. Some have adhered strictly to teaching behavioural principles, whilst others have moved more toward broader approaches to child rearing and the strengthening of parenting skills. Some have consciously tried to share basic principles and techniques with parents on the assumption that this would promote more generalized parental awareness and ability to solve or prevent future difficulties themselves.

Most include discussion of normal development and typical developments in groups that are disabled or have learning or behavioural difficulties. These vary according to the nature of the child and the disability. For young children with developmental delay, emphasis is on general sensori-motor development, whereas with older children topics such as language, play and behaviour disorders are more common. Some concentrate upon specific topics such as reading, sexuality or drug abuse. Regardless of the topic, most workshops train parents in management strategies and usually take the opportunity to provide information about local and national resources.

Apart from therapeutic groups and educational–behavioural workshops, a third type is largely aimed at providing information. These generally consist of a series of lectures (sometimes with films and demonstrations) followed by discussion. They cover a broad range of topics including the causes and nature of various disabilities, types of treatment, services available, employment prospects, etc. If school-based they often focus on the school aims and curriculum areas, and upon the role of associated services such as speech therapy and educational psychology. Their main functions are to provide information to a large number of people, to open up areas for discussion and to motivate or inspire thinking and interest. They have the advantage of attracting a range of parents, including those who may be shy or unwilling to attend small discussion groups where they are expected to participate. Shy parents who do not feel socially competent and articulate, or who are uneasy with 'experts', can attend large meetings without 'being put in the limelight'. However, such meetings cannot cater for individual needs and many attenders may feel that the experience was not worthwhile. Similarly, discussions that take place may be biased and only represent the views of those parents willing to debate publicly.

The distinction between therapeutic groups aimed principally at providing emotional support and aiding adjustment, and educational–behavioural workshops, aimed at practical support and skills, is largely academic. The few evaluated studies available indicate that parents generally do not make the distinction between emotional and practical help that professionals do (Key, Hooper & Ballard, 1979; Sloper, Cunningham & Arnjlsdottir, 1983). Parents are concerned with immediate needs and appreciate any helpful solution. Practical training is seen as highly supportive, and having someone to talk to about anxieties is seen as very practical in helping them to help the child and themselves. Except in extreme cases, parents are more likely to take part in an activity if they perceive it has some practical relevance. They generally endorse training opportunities as a priority whereas professionals often feel that parents need counselling for emotional and adjustment difficulties. It is sometimes argued that parents are reluctant to seek out counselling for emotional needs either because they perceive this as an abnormality in themselves and with an associated stigma or because they have little experience or conception of this area of help.

This latter point highlights a major problem in evaluating approaches. Unless parents have experienced different approaches they can only evaluate the one experienced against nothing. If the approach does meet some needs they are likely to agree that it is supportive. Furthermore, most approaches rely upon parents attending voluntarily and most evaluations are based on those still present at the end of the activity. Several studies have indicated that regardless of the approach used, parents from higher socio-economic groups tend to be more likely to enrol and complete courses. One of the few studies to look at parents who do not enrol on courses (McConkey & McEvoy, 1984) found that these mothers of mentally handicapped pre-school children felt they were already doing as good a job as possible as parents, did not share the values of the course and were less actively involved in play with their child. Thus throughout this chapter the reader should keep in mind that the evaluations may be biased toward those parents who find value in the activity. To provide the most useful information about groups, the findings of published studies are summarized under a number of headings.

Venue

Parent groups have been held in hospitals, clinics, social service residences, schools, adult training centres, colleges, church halls, public houses, hostels and homes. Apart from the suggestion that college or university settings may be threatening to some parents and homes produce more informal and relaxed interactions, there does not appear to be any particularly favoured venue.

However, if it is familiar and easily accessible to parents, then more appear to attend. It is important to provide comfortable and adequate accommodation. Parents will evaluate the course and hence themselves and their child from many impressions including the appearance of the venue, the organization and the quality of materials. Parent groups who have met in hotels and public houses have reported that this appears to speed up the creation of a relaxed and convivial atmosphere and that fathers are more likely to attend. Nevertheless, such places may be inappropriate for some parents for religious or cultural reasons.

Size of Group

For groups aimed at information-giving only, size does not appear to be critical. It becomes critical when the aim is to meet individual needs and change behaviour. This requires considerable time for discussion, and small groups are required. The most appropriate size for discussion groups is about 8 to 12 parents representing 5 to 8 families. This provides a sufficient variety of needs, perspectives and shared experiences, and yet allows the group to remain manageable, whilst coping with absences.

Number of Sessions

These have ranged from 3 to over 60, with the 'therapeutic' groups tending to show the greater variation in number of sessions. The average is somewhere between 6 and 12. Most lecture/information oriented approaches are around 6. For small groups, the first two or three sessions are required to established relationships and an acceptable way of group functioning. More than 10 to 12 sessions usually places a too great demand on commitments for regular attendance and can overload the amount of learning and training expected.

Time-Interval Between Sessions

Weekly sessions are typical. This allows for time to think about and try out suggestions, collect observations, etc. It is important that the interval is long enough for parents to conduct practical exercises and consolidate or apply the learning. It should not be so long that, if they find they have not understood or are not getting results, they have to wait before they can consult the group. Furthermore, frequent contact with the group and new

ideas are necessary to maintain an impetus and feeling of change.
Two weekly intervals or more are likely to endanger this. Some
workshops use weekly sessions for the first approximately two-
thirds of the course, but then move to fortnightly, then once every
three weeks as a 'weaning' process. This is based on the assumption that having found the meetings highly supportive a sudden
cessation may be undesirable. Information oriented groups appear
to be less dependent on the interval between sessions. However,
parents seem more able to organize their family routines around
regular weekly or monthly meetings.

Practical Aspects

Careful consideration has to be given to the background of parents
and child and the aims of the workshop. Single parent families
or parents of children with severe behavioural difficulties are more
likely to encounter child-minding problems. If held in the even-
ings, more fathers attend. Organizers should also consider local
travel conditions, such as rush hours, train and bus times and
the closing time of local work places. During the winter, dark
nights and bad weather may inhibit attendance.

Length and Structure of Sessions

The average session is between one-and-a-half to two hours. A
two-hour session appears preferable since it usually includes time
for tea or coffee at the beginning, middle or the end. This is noted
as being important for informal parent contact and often leads
to social support networks being generated. For some workshops,
the first part of the session presents general principles, using
lectures, films or demonstrations, and then small groups meet
for discussion. Once the basic information has been given in the
earlier sessions, the objectives move toward consolidation and
practice and an emphasis on individual problems or tasks. Consequently, later sessions are used almost exclusively for small
group discussion. Where the workshop is based on small numbers
with no outside speakers, all sessions have tended to use the
discussion format. Most workshops include a final discussion
session, often with a panel of speakers and an evaluation with
a 'where to go from here' session.

Group Composition

Usually there are more mothers than fathers, though this varies according to when the group meets and possibly the nature of the group. Fathers' attendance at evening meetings is high, especially if emphasis is given to the advantages of both parents being present. More fathers appear willing to attend workshops with clearly stated objectives that appear practical, as opposed to less defined support groups. They are also more irregular than mothers in attending the latter and this may reflect different needs, with mothers, for example, needing to get out of the house and talk and fathers having more opportunities for this. Thus, groups that meet both practical and emotional needs are more likely to attract both parents.

Some groups encourage siblings and grandparents to attend as well, but restriction has to be made on the number of members representing one child to avoid imbalance. Groups have also been organized specifically for siblings and less frequently for grandparents. These focus primarily on information and emotional support rather than on training in educational or behavioural methods, although the more successful appear to aim at providing information about the child to help understanding, practical ways of interacting with the handicapped person and/or dealing with embarrassing situations.

Reports suggest that parents prefer to be in a group where their children have a similar disability or set of difficulties and are of similar age. Initially, this may relate to a perceived identity and empathy with other members, but in later sessions reflects the importance of ensuring that the content of groups is compatible with current individual needs. Thus, it is well worth assessing likely needs prior to composing the group.

Many groups appear to have a bias toward higher socio-economic class parents which may largely be due to practical problems in attending. It may also reflect the way parents construe their relationship with professionals and suggests a need for considerable effort in establishing relationships prior to the workshops. There does not, however, appear to be any difference in the parents' ability to benefit from workshops or their satisfaction according to social class or educational background. The exception is when parents are themselves mentally handicapped and require considerably more tailor-made programmes and individual help.

Lectures with written materials and/or note taking is an academic mode of learning that may not be within the experience of many parents. Thus demonstrations, films and small discussion groups can be more appropriate and successful. Indeed, there is some consensus that written material has limited value and that parent discussion groups are really the only satisfactory way of passing on information, even for topics such as school philosophy and goals. Summaries of talks and information handouts are, however, useful for reference by parents after the meetings and can also avoid later disputes over what was said.

Finally, little attention has been given to the characteristics or motives of parents who do not enroll in groups. Often they are labelled 'apathetic' and 'disinterested', but this is no explanation and is a form of 'pathological' thinking. There may be many other reasons for not attending, such as transport difficulties, work commitments, illness or organization of baby sitters. Most of these problems can be solved once identified. In cases where parents are shy of groups and 'experts', then personal contact prior to the group meeting may reduce the perceived threat.

There is some evidence to indicate that while the professional may believe that the course would benefit the parent and child, the parent may not share this opinion. They may believe, for example, that there is little they can do to influence the child's development, and therefore they will not see the course as relevant to them. Such parents may be encouraged by clearly stating the rationale and objectives of the workshop prior to it beginning. Again in initial courses this can be helped if a range of needs and aims are met, some of which appear relevant to different parents. It is even more useful to negotiate with parents prior to the workshop. Often, especially with parents who have had unsatisfactory educational experiences or dealings with professionals, a long process of confidence building is necessary and regular contacts may be required. With exceptions, however, there is generally little difficulty in finding sufficient numbers of parents. A range of advertising methods have been used including local newspapers, radio and television programmes, posters and local health and social services. Groups based in particular schools or centres tend to restrict membership to the parents of the children attending. Where the aim concerns major transitions, (e.g. nursery to school, school to adult centre or employment) joint workshops between the two establishments, which include parents from both, have many advantages.

Leaders, Tutors and Lecturers

Many workshops have been organized by psychologists (clinical and educational), but more frequently they are run by combinations of professionals including teachers, community nurses, speech, physio- and occupational therapists, medical practitioners and social workers. Most reports do not state whether the group leaders have had training in counselling techniques or running small groups but all have some specialism in the field of disability. Some reports do note that leaders were chosen for their ability to communicate and create empathic relationships, but more often they depend upon availability.

The leaders' ability to run groups and establish relationships and the ways parents construe the professionals involved, appear to be key factors. For example, some reports of groups organized by psychologists note that the presence of centre and school staff as group leaders can inhibit parents from voicing concerns and issues which they feel reflect upon themselves or the staff. Also, especially if under any stress, parents may want to know what to do and need to feel confident that the 'experts' know what to do. They may construe the school or centre staff as having a definite body of correct knowledge and that their information can apply equally to all the children and families. Consequently, professionals can find themselves in the ambiguous situation of being expected to have answers and yet, in the context of the group discussion and workshops, attempting to share their knowledge and lack of knowledge with the aim of helping parents develop their own problem-solving skills. This perceived uncertainty can produce feelings of ambivalence or incompetence in both parents and staff. Unless prepared, staff can feel threatened and may try to give hasty solutions which have a high probability of failing. This then damages parental confidence and the relationship. It is important, therefore, to discuss this danger and parental expectations openly in the early sessions. Such discussion is an aspect of the skill of immediacy described in Chapter 6. For many staff who have little experience or training in groupwork with parents, prior preparation by way of their own workshop is needed to consider content, structure and interactive and organizational skills.

Throughout the workshop, staff meetings between sessions enable progress to be evaluated and changes to be made in subsequent sessions. Such meetings also provide support for the staff. Some workshops and groups have used two leaders for each discussion group, so that, for sessions exploring feelings, one may act largely as the director of the group, the other as observer noting parental reactions. Others have alternated the roles or assume control when appropriate according to their background. This appears to be a useful approach in that more individual needs are met and the leaders provide support for each other.

It is important in using lectures that outside speakers are well briefed and that their talk interlocks well with the aims and style

of the workshop. A written factual and practical summary should
be provided for later reference in the discussion groups or individually. Several reports have noted parent dissatisfaction with
poorly presented talks and/or summaries that are long, technical,
and complicated. There is some suggestion that parent attendance
may drop in following sessions if too many lectures are like this.
It is unfortunate that most reports of groups fail to note attendance
figures and/or in their follow-up evaluation do not contact parents
who drop out and discover why.

Evaluation

Since many groups are service and not research oriented, evaluation of specific aspects and results are not common. Few have
comparison groups, long-term follow-up or objective measures.
However, there is a consensus of findings from both impressionis-
tic and objective data.

(1) Support   Parents rate the support given by talking to other
parents as one of the greatest benefits. This includes emotional
support from, for example, realizing that other parents have similar problems, and practical support in seeing how others have
solved or are attempting to solve problems. Interestingly,
approaches which have been largely behaviourally oriented have
often concluded that this is an important aspect needing more
consideration, whilst the more reflective, therapeutic groups
report the need to provide practical suggestions in management.
Thus, since most approaches now have the dual aims of support
and training, they structure the sessions to allow maximum informal contact between parents and discussion groups. Some
specifically begin workshops with discussions on reactions, feelings and problems before introducing more behavioural content.
Professionals also note how their experience in such groups has
improved their own understanding and given them support in
their work.

(2) Confidence   Most studies report that parents gain increased
confidence in interacting with their child. This appears to come
from the support given, the realization that other parents have
similar difficulties and the acquisition of new skills, which have
been applied and seen to work.

(3) Knowledge and Skills   The majority of parents do gain knowledge and skills, particularly in their ability to observe, to understand behaviour change and child development and to apply these

to their children. Often parents note the most important element was learning how to observe and interpret the child's behaviour which then gave them some idea of what to do.

A minority may react against the structural elements, since for example, recording behaviour during teaching or play sessions can be unreal, too formal and distant: 'When I play with him I think how do I record this and so I stop playing naturally. Sometimes I think I won't do something because I can't record it'. As discussed in previous chapters, parents do not work like professionals and rely more on opportunity and spontaneity. Hence, when requesting that parents keep records, these should be as uncomplicated as possible and well designed (e.g. Newson & Hipgrave, 1982).

(4) *Positive Changes in Child Behaviour*   These are frequently reported. The rare evaluations of 'therapeutic-counselling' groups report a majority of parents having improved child–parent interaction (Hornby & Singh, 1983). In workshops, parent and professional ratings show improvements in behaviour problems and in the acquisition of new skills. However, short workshops appear to be more effective in changing behaviour for younger mentally handicapped children, below eight or so years, or those with less severe behaviour disorders. Little change is found in profoundly handicapped children, older severely handicapped children or those with severe disorders (Cunningham & Jeffree, 1975; Firth, 1982). Interestingly, some school-based programmes catering for the whole range, find that it is the parents of the older mentally handicapped children without major management problems who are more likely to stop attending. Presumably their needs are not as pressing or obvious and are not met by the workshops. Yet parents of profoundly handicapped and severely disturbed children often maintain attendance, possibly because they need the support, despite the lack of success in applying techniques. Several reports conclude that for such parents a home-based programme with more professional involvement with the child is necessary. In fact some parents have such severe current problems with their child that they pressurize the group leaders for specific, immediate counselling and are unwilling or unable to work through general principles. They are unable to step beyond the immediate day-to-day needs into areas of general concept discussion appropriate to the group. This illustrates the problem of meeting individual needs in a group context. Opportunities for individual counselling may relieve the pressure and the parent may then still benefit from group support. Occasionally parents also find it difficult to work with their own child whilst developing

skills. Opportunities for working with another child can help resolve this by allowing the parent to reformulate ideas and behaviours in relative safety, free from past experience and their high attachment to their own child.

(5) Long-Term Effects   A beneficial long term effect is that parents may maintain the contacts made; some even form self-help groups. School or centre based workshops have also noted increased and improved parent contacts including more direct involvement in educational aspects of their child's life, more efficient communications and less conflict with staff.

In terms of applying the techniques learnt to new behaviours during the post-workshop period, the majority of parents do not maintain the same level of assessment, planning and regular teaching sessions (Harris, 1983). Instead, they generally apply the learning more spontaneously and opportunistically. For children with more severe handicaps and behaviour problems, many parents find it hard to apply the techniques independently and some never try. These results are specific to persistent learning or behaviour difficulties and reflect the need for long-term contact. However, where parents have successfully attended a workshop, they appear to require less professional help in dealing with new problems, and this suggests they have internalized the concepts and approaches and merely need additional support to initiate new activity. Most studies of parents whose children have persistent learning difficulties and handicaps conclude that there is the need for follow-up sessions to maintain parent activity.

(6) Group Failure   Few reports are available of groups or workshops that fail, since unfortunately these tend not to be published. Thus, the picture presented here may be optimistic. However, failures appear to relate to poor organization, including lack of attention to detail like travel or transport difficulties, compatibility of venue, poor matching of parent needs and abilities with content, presentation and characteristics of group leaders.

(7) New Families   One disadvantage of workshops is that they depend upon sufficient numbers of parents with similar needs at the same time. Typically, the first workshops in a given area have found sufficient numbers of parents available. New families needing similar support and guidance, however, appear all the time and cannot wait for sufficient numbers to accrue to form a group. Also, with the increase in early home support programmes, parents may independently receive guidance on educational and behavioural aspects. It is necessary, therefore, to consider how workshops will fit into the ongoing support service. Nevertheless, this constraint is less likely to affect groups which

are oriented largely to support and more informal approaches for information exchange and guidance.

Concluding Comments

Overall, parent groups and workshops appear to form a particularly useful and effective method of working with parents. It is a flexible way of meeting a wide range of needs and can be applied to an array of topics. A key principle is active involvement of parents through discussion and practical activities. For example, even if the aim is to inform parents of aspects of the curriculum, it can be far more meaningful and enjoyable if they participate in the actual exercises in which their children engage, than if they listen passively.

Successful groups and workshops are characterized by:

(i)   *Meeting parent needs.* This can be achieved by joint decision making on content. Circulating a rationale and set of ideas with a request for parents to indicate their interests and make suggestions, not only increases likely relevance but also signals to parents the desire for a partnership by saying, 'You are the consumer, tell us what you want'.

(ii) *Fitting in with parent resources.* Negotiate time, dates, travel arrangements, likely skills and abilities required to participate and selection for appropriate groups depending on their needs and child. Some parents will respond to a letter, others require a telephone call or visit.

(iii) *Conveying the impression of value.* Ensure that the venue and all materials, whether letters, posters, notes, pamphlets or visual aids, are of good quality to avoid giving the impression that the exercise is not important.

(iv) *Well organized and planned.* (a) Provide parents with clear statements of rationale, aims, structure and requirements before enrolement. Satisfaction is closely related to expectations, and so it is essential to convey what to expect and *what not to expect.* Some workshops use a mutually designed contract between parents and professionals which is signed by both partners and it has been found that this is positively related to attendance and completing work assignments. (b) Remind parents a few days before the meetings begin. (c) Start and end the meetings as punctually as possible. (d) Ensure the venue is appropriate. (e) Take opportunities to make information available and use displays. (f) Have tea or coffee available on time. These all convey a feeling of value and the importance attached to the exercise. They signal competence and reduce likely conflict. They make the parent feel welcomed and respected. They demonstrate a positive attitude.

(v) *Quality of staff.* (a) Select good speakers and brief them. (b) Train group leaders and hold regular discussions to evaluate progress. (c) Keep records of parents' comments and be prepared to adapt workshops to meet expressed needs.

Recent Developments

There has been a move in some countries for parent workshops which focus on the advocacy role of parents or on parents acting as counsellors to other parents, often called Parent-to-Parent schemes. Those with counselling as the focus begin with discussion of the parents' feelings and emotional adjustment, followed by training in counselling skills. The last sessions deal with organization, such as establishing contact with professional referral sources, publicity management and finance, and they also provide information on local and national resources and methods of referral to other services. The advocacy oriented courses focus on (i) helping parents develop skills for interacting with professionals on a personal and/or group basis, (ii) methods for evaluating local services and (iii) information on the structure of services, including chains of command, legal rights and appeal procedures. These courses are generally initiated by parents or parent–professional collaboration, but they require professional help in organization, content and teaching. Whilst there is often professional resistance to these developments, they are logical extensions of the principles of parent–professional partnership and accountability.

If we accept that parent-to-parent support can be particularly fruitful, and even more effective than professional involvement in some areas, then it is necessary to provide basic skills. The professionals who feel threatened by such developments must ask whether it is their status that they are defending or the quality of service. Similarly, the threat of parents acting in an evaluative and advocacy role may be more imagined than real. A number of studies have found, for example, that in discussions between parents and teachers there is surprisingly little discrepancy between them in terms of attitudes and aims, especially when each attempts to understand the other's position. Indeed, in her description of setting up a parent self-help group, Grace Woods (1981) noted that such groups are more successful if parents are fundamentally happy with professional services, because the group becomes something more than a complaint organization to release aggression and tension. Furthermore, parents do appear to gain a deep satisfaction at being able to both give and receive help.

Individual Support

Home-based approaches to working with individual parents vary enormously from traditional visits by health visitors and social workers to regular weekly visits over years by a member of a multidisciplinary team (Aplin & Pugh, 1983; Pugh, 1982). These have also included peripatetic teachers of the visually or learning impaired children, home tuition, and parent–teacher liaison. We will focus on support programmes designed specifically to meet the main needs of parents and to provide guidance and training in working with the pre-school child with special needs. The content of such programmes is similar to the workshop and group approaches and range from those which are mainly oriented to providing emotional support and strengthening parenting skills to those which are focused almost exclusively on techniques to teach the child new behaviours or control behaviour difficulties.

The period covered by home-based programmes ranges from 2 to 3 months to several years. Visiting rates vary from weekly to 8 weekly intervals in most programmes, with those oriented to more general support using flexible visiting schedules which are negotiated with parents, depending on their current needs.

The relative advantages and disadvantages of home-based and centre-based approaches have received much attention (Gray & Wandersman, 1980), but what is often missed is the relationship between the two in terms of the aims of the support programme and the parents' current needs. Home-based programmes cater for parents unwilling or unable to travel to centres and so increase the likelihood of reaching families most at risk who may not attend centres or who drop out of groups. In handicapping conditions discovered at birth this is seen as essential in order to reduce additional stress in the early period of adjustment, which could result from travel to centres and having to meet other people. For some, meeting other parents can be useful during the early traumatic period, but for many it may be overwhelming. Later, however, home-visiting alone is a disadvantage for those parents, who would then benefit from support groups.

Two broad phases of early home-support are discernible. The first encompasses infancy and toddlerhood (from 0 – 3 years) built around a home-based approach and dependent upon local services. As we have already discussed, the early period after the diagnosis, whenever it is made, is a formative one when parents are rapidly reconstructing models of themselves and the child, and having to learn new skills. It may be a particularly critical phase and have long term implications for the development of relationships between family members and between parents and professionals. It requires, therefore, concentrated time from both professionals and parents, and it is highly individual. For these reasons, home-based support appears most appropriate. Furthermore the most constant environment for infants and toddlers is the home and local community and so this should be the focus for services.

The second phase begins at the time the child is moving into the larger community with involvement in pre-school facilities. As noted, this is a major life-cycle event for most families and can be stressful. Parents have to make emotional and organizational adjustments; the school or centre staff begin to play an increasing role in the development of programmes and provision of parent support. The home visitor has to help this transition, and a central role will be to liaise with these establishments. Both the establishment staff and home visitor will need to have this role clearly outlined in their job specifications if they are not going to be faced with uncertainty and lack of resources.

Apart from providing for more intensive work, home-based approaches have the advantage of increasing the likelihood that individual family needs will be met. They offer the possibility of assessing the child's environment (social and material) as well as family resources, social support networks and socio-cultural factors more accurately.

In centre-based programmes dealing with a large number of children, the amount of time for exclusive work with parents and child is often reduced and other aspects, such as the parent joining in group discussions can intrude. Thus it is often less easy to give individual guidance or correction in using therapy or teaching methods. On the other hand, the more the professional is dependent upon the parent for information about the child and how particular teaching strategies are working, as in workshop approaches where the child is never seen, the more likely they are to share their skills and ideas with the parent and to keep the focus of the work clearly on the parent. One danger inherent in working with individual families is that the home visitor or therapist begins to focus on the child, demonstrating what parents should do in a somewhat cook-book fashion. This is unlikely to produce long-lasting changes in parental behaviour or to support their feelings of competence.

Home-based approaches also increase the prospect of establishing a fruitful relationship with parents, since they are on familiar ground, in control of events and therefore less likely to feel threatened. This can, however, be an initial disadvantage with parents who construe the professional as assessing the home and making adverse judgements. Such dangers can be overcome to some extent by making the first meeting outside the home, by making appointments so that parents are prepared for the visit, or by a telephone conversation. The telephone can provide a comforting physical barrier yet at the same time a more personal or individual dialogue. However, it can be intrusive and one should begin by asking if it is convenient to talk at that time. The explicit aim of such initial contacts is to show that the professional 'is not that type of person' and to explain the aims of the visit.

Some home-based visitors have encountered similar problems in relation to their base. Those based in special schools, for example, often find parents less willing to participate because, it is thought, they associate the visitor with severe handicap or inevitable special schooling. This is obviously most pertinent in the early pre-school years, but can equally be expected for parents of children attending primary schools. If the advisory person brought in is based at a special school, the parent may construe this as suggesting the services feel the child should attend such a school.

Of course, such reactions are closely related to the child's special needs and handicaps. Advisory services such as those for visual or auditory handicap, speech or physio-therapy are generally understood by parents. Most recognize and appreciate the specialized service, seen as it is, to relate to their child's special condition. Difficulties are more likely to arise in less discernible conditions such as developmental delay, even when associated with well recognized conditions like Down's Syndrome. Because of the greater uncertainty and possible stigma attached to mental handicap, many parents appear to have a more difficult task in adjustment and developing workable constructs.

In the early years, therefore, many parents are sensitive to the connotations of the services and are often less happy to relate to those construed as specializing in severe retardation, unless they recognize that their child falls into this category and requires such services. Consequently, it appears that they are more willing to develop a relationship with services and establishments that they perceive as dealing with a wide range of special needs. Attendance at centres and transition to pre-school facilities are therefore facilitated the more the parents perceive them as 'normal' or integrated rather than separated. There is an anomaly however, because parents also find support by being in contact with other parents of children who have similar conditions and needs. Thus centre-based programmes can deter some parents and need to consider carefully what image they project to parents.

We will now consider four examples of recent approaches in the United Kingdom. They have been chosen because they (1) are documented and have received some evaluation; (2) reflect a range from an educational to a supportive orientation; and (3) focus upon a range of needs from those of the child to those of the family as a whole.

The Portage Approach

Perhaps the best known home-based intervention is the Portage Guide to Early Education (Cameron, 1982; Dessent, 1984). This was originally developed in a rural area in Wisconsin, U.S.A., centred on the town of Portage. It involves weekly home visits of 1 to 2 hours by a community worker who deals with 6 to 10 families. Home visitors come from a range of professionals including community nurses, health visitors, teachers, therapists, psychologists and some non-professionals. Most approaches have found that a short training programme is all that is initially necessary. The Portage method has a one week training programme focusing on the use of prepared guides and principles of behavioural change and early development.

The main purpose of each visit is to help the parent (usually the mother in day-time programmes) to select and set appropriate short-term goals expected to be achieved within one or two weeks, and to devise an appropriate teaching strategy. To this end they are trained to use a developmental checklist which covers the development between birth and 5 to 6 years in the areas of socialization and language and also cognitive, self-help and motor skills. For each item on the checklist there is a corresponding card which lists suggested activities and methods designed to help the child reach the goal, which is the next step in his/her development. Together with the well presented package of curricula cards and checklist, there is an accompanying guide for parents which explains the methods and basic rationale for the approach. The home visitor assists the parent to make the assessment, to select the target behaviour and to state it in behavioural terms. This is then noted on an activity chart together with a method of recording progress. The method and materials are then worked out and demonstrated with the child, and written directions put on the activity chart for reference. The major methods taught to parents are reinforcement, modelling, shaping and prompting, correction procedures and consideration of aids and materials. At the next visit the home visitor reviews progress using the recording chart, modifies the programme if necessary and/or selects new target behaviours. The number of target behaviours selected for each week varies according to the ability of the child but it is generally between 1 and 4, and they are taught in short daily teaching sessions. Apart from the appropriateness of the behaviour in terms of the child's level of development, target behaviours are selected in terms of being most immediately functional for the child and for being areas of specific weakness.

Again, in common with other programmes, the home visitors meet on a frequent and regular basis with a specialist organizer or multidisciplinary team to discuss progress, difficulties encountered and new strategies. This provides support for staff, which many approaches have noted as necessary to cope with the heterogeneity of needs and the danger of staff becoming disillusioned and disheartened, a particular danger for those spending most of their time with severe disabilities where there is high uncertainty and limited success, especially if isolated from colleagues. Such meetings also provide on-going training and staff development, as well as evaluation of the service as a whole.

A well demonstrated advantage of the Portage approach is that the methods and materials are relatively easy to understand and to apply by staff and parents alike. This provides a structure and direction which increase confidence and, in turn, involvement with the child.

An original aim of the Portage approach, again common to other programmes, was that as parents become increasingly skilled in planning and carrying out programmes, the home visitor's role would gradually change, becoming more that of a consultant, providing advice, support and encouragement to maintain parents' competence and their feelings of self-confidence. It has been suggested, however, that the nature of the materials may lead some home visitors to neglect this aim. Thus, it has to be clearly emphasized in initial training and evaluated regularly in order to avoid the service becoming largely prescriptive.

The Portage guides were originally developed for children with moderate developmental delay and without obvious functional difficulties (e.g. vision, hearing, co-ordination). The content is also largely derived from activities used in standardized assessments for normal development. Their applicability to more seriously handicapped children and the functionality of some items has been questioned and will be discussed later. Several investigations have found that progress is more likely with children from environmentally deprived backgrounds and those with moderate delay, and some services (e.g. the South Glamorgan Home Advisory Service) have found it necessary to modify the guides particularly for more severely handicapped children. Reports from this **well evaluated service also highlight the need for home visitors** to encompass areas such as family adjustment and conceptions of handicapping conditions (Revill & Blunden, 1979).

The major criticisms aimed at the Portage and similar approaches are, therefore, that they do not give sufficient attention to the social and emotional development of the child and the fact that much early learning is mediated through the interactions between the child and the social environment. In the same vein, there is no training of home visitors to look at, be concerned with and help in the well-being of the whole family. Thus the approach is highly child-focused and primarily directed at improving the performance of the children on behaviour typically found in early developmental tests.

The Honeylands Project

The Honeylands Project is one example of a comprehensive service for families with severely handicapped children commencing from birth (Rubissow, 1976). Primarily a paediatric care service based on a children's hospital in Exeter, it provided residential care for short term relief. A multidisciplinary team was available to carry out assessments and to provide therapy, family support and play-group facilities. It was noted that in the first stage of recognition of handicap, families might adjust better if the support service was home-based. The home visitors that were used came from all disciplines of the team and also included a trained parent. They were matched to families in relation to the needs of the child, the characteristics of the family and the qualities of the visitor.

The aim was twofold: (i) to establish a practical service providing emotional support and information, and (ii) to train parents in methods, similar to those described above, to facilitate the child's development and functioning. A clear role of the home visitor was to integrate the advice of the team and act as the mediator between the service and family; this is a role similar to that of the 'named person' advocated by the Warnock Report. Weekly visits took place in the first year and then by arrangement with the families. The aim, as noted above, was to reduce the dependency on the visitor as the parent gained skills and adjusted.

One interesting early finding was that the development programme planned by the team in the centre for the child could rarely be implemented in the home (Rayner, 1978). This arose from the team's lack of knowledge of the parents' resources or their emotional difficulties in adjusting to the child's condition and not only reinforces the importance of a home-based service, but also the need for the service to be flexible and reactive to parent needs, avoiding a too prescriptive, child-focused approach. Also, because of the slow progress made by many children, they found, in common with other services, that it was necessary to break down developmental tasks into minute steps and to reassess the psychological and functional importance of selected behaviours for the child in order to increase their own understanding and awareness and that of the parents. In short, unless the selected goal is seen as worthwhile, it is unlikely that parents or professionals will invest resources in attaining it.

Similarly, emphasis was given to providing knowledge for parents in order to help them understand the child, to interpret his/her behaviour and to appreciate the consequences and future implications. The service included access to support groups. It was suggested that these, and the provision of information and support, were pre-requisites for coping with practical day-to-day problems and facilitating the child's development. As noted earlier, these two aspects are closely interrelated; the provision of practical advice to assist development can act as a powerful therapeutic support and can be developed in tandem with other aspects of counselling and support.

The Honeylands service is one of a few which have evaluated the effects of their efforts beyond parental satisfaction and child gains. Comparison of the mothers with a similar group receiving traditional services indicated that those involved in the Honeylands Project were less likely to show signs of stress, depression or worry and generally had more positive outlooks and attitudes in the early years at least (Burden, 1980).

Three mothers (Key, Hooper & Ballard, 1979) involved with the Honeylands Project also published an article on their observations. This is unusual, as most evaluations are mediated via the professional. Apart from evaluating the needs of parents they present a lengthy list of characteristics and responsibilities of the home visitor. These include: understanding the whole problem of daily and future stresses faced by all family members; teaching the parent to observe and understand the child's behaviour; building an honest, trusting relationship in which the parent can confide feelings about the child and family; and being sensitive to the changing professional and parent relationship which they argue includes being able to accurately define the professional role. Clearly, this supports professional evaluations that home visitors have to have a more extensive role and not merely be focused on teaching the child.

Educational Home Visiting Schemes

Programmes for children from disadvantaged backgrounds have been more common that those for organic conditions. Whereas the latter represent the whole range of socio-economic groupings, the former are largely concerned with families in lower groupings. Much of the information available is from the Headstart movement in the United States (The Consortium for Longitudinal Studies, 1983; Lazar & Darlington, 1982; Slaughter, 1983), but it should be remembered that these usually deal with very impoverished families, often from black communities. It is possible, therefore, that there are cultural differences which may not make them directly transferable to Britain. These programmes aim to compensate for the perceived lack of learning opportunities and relevant social models which appear to lead to low expectations, low self-confidence and negative attitudes toward services and education. Many of these programmes recognize that the attitudes and aspirations of the parents themselves have been similarly influenced and so form a self-perpetuating cycle. Thus, some have specifically aimed at involving parents in order to change their feelings of competence and their aspirations for themselves and their children.

The degree of parent involvement ranges from minimal to that of acting in decision-making roles about the nature and content of the programmes, as well as learning methods to help the child. Several reviews have concluded that the greater the degree of parental involvement, the less the likelihood of gains being 'washed out' in later years. In fact, the most beneficial results appear to be associated with programmes where parents had a decision-making role which, in turn, influenced their learning roles. The inclusion of parents in decision-making roles may indicate that such programmes aimed at a partnership relationship which, in turn, fostered the growth of self-competence.

Over recent years there has been a considerable shift in conception about the enduring effects of early intervention. Initially, most evaluations focused on psychometric measures but when these were largely found to be small or washed-out over the years, emphasis was given to other outcomes.

Long term benefits in scholastic attainment have been small, but more Headstart children have tended to remain in mainstream education rather than special provision. The factors which appear to be most related to the endurance of gains are the attitudes and aspirations of the child and the parents. The process seems to be that of building up in the child positive ways of construing teachers and him/herself through the acquisition of skill and knowledge. This gives an initial advantage when entering school and decreases the likelihood of deterioration. This in turn influences the ways in which both teachers and parents construe the child and hence interact with her/him. Other long term benefits have been indicated in terms of mother–parent interaction patterns. Mothers encouraged to develop a more democratic communication style with their child appear to have more active synchronized interactions in later years and the children are more likely to express themselves. Such findings are only gradually emerging, though there are still many methodological problems in determining precisely what the effects and antecedents are.

As with programmes for more handicapped children, the approaches range from those which are highly structured and teacher-directed to those which are more open-ended, emphasizing child initiative. Short-term gains are found in both, but there is some suggestion that the latter may have longer lasting effects. Nevertheless, all beneficial approaches are characterized by clear objectives and good organization.

Home visiting and community education services in Britain have followed similar lines. Woodhead (1976) has reviewed this work and Midwinter (1977) has described efforts made in Educational Priority Areas. An example of a home-based approach is the Lothian Regional Educational Home Visiting Scheme, described by Raven (1980). The main aims were to improve cognitive development and language in two to three year old children from deprived areas and to influence parental attitudes, interests and involvement with their child by emphasizing the nature and importance of the mother's role in promoting the education of the child. The home teachers were all primary or nursery trained. They were based in local schools and attended short induction courses prior to the home visits. Each visited 10 to 12 families, referred by social workers or schools, for about one hour a week for an average period of around 9 months.

They began by working directly with the child on activities selected to facilitate cognitive development, providing materials such as books, jigsaws and picture games. Gradually, the mother was encouraged to participate in order to promote her self-confidence and involvement with the child. It was assumed that this more positive attitude would then communicate itself to the child. The educational home visitor also initiated out-of-home activities with groups of children and parents.

The scheme was interesting in that the home visitors were given considerable flexibility in how to develop their own style and which aspects to emphasize. The evaluation by Raven, clearly indicates that this was influenced by their model of cognitive development and of the parental role. Some emphasized teaching of colours, classification, sequencing and relationships; others focused upon the enhancement of the child's ability to perceive and think clearly and learning to learn. Similarly, strong divergence was found between home visitors in the extent to which they believed that promoting mothers' cognitive processes and feelings of self-confidence in dealing with their own problems would facilitate the development of the child. In this, the study encapsulates many current issues and is well worth further enquiry.

It is unfortunate that the evaluation was not built into the initial design of the scheme and many methodological flaws have been recognized by the researchers. Even so it indicates that the scheme generally increased child attainments and competence and improved parental attitudes and expectations. It suggested that the children were better prepared for school by experiencing teachers and teaching in the home, and this promoted better adjustment. Family relationships also appeared to improve with mothers more able to initiate activities for the child and so keep them amused and 'out of mischief'. It is also suggested that parents were more likely to take the child's behaviour seriously and reason with him/her. Parent–professional and home/school relationships appeared to improve as parents felt more confident in dealing with teachers. As a result they were more likely to act as advocates to promote the child at school and to interact with the teachers. The out-of-home activities apparently reduced mothers' feelings of isolation and depression by extending the social support network, and they were more likely to call for help to prevent crises.

Interestingly, the home visitors and the schools also changed. Their perception of parents altered, from construing them as incapable and apathetic to seeing the families as under stress from many sources which they could, at least, partially, influence. It is also suggested that the teachers became more aware that education is about facilitating the growth of competence rather than solely transmitting knowledge and skills. Presumably, this prompts teachers to reflect on their own role. Are they to act only within their professional area of expertise (i.e. to teach) or to what extent should they take on broader functions of dealing with family issues and counselling for emotional or social difficulties. This issue of the role and job specification of home visitors has received little attention and needs more research, particularly as all the results were not positive, in that some parents appeared to become less competent and more dependent. It was suggested that this may have arisen from undue stress on the parental teaching function and excessively high expectations about the child's school success as a result of the parents' efforts. It was also noted that where home visitors largely showed the parents what to do and presented themselves as highly competent and more capable than parents, this may have reduced the parents' self-image.

Self-Help and Volunteer Schemes

The usefulness of non-professional support has been a common theme in many approaches and appears to provide an important addition with its own unique contribution. 'Non-professional' support is, by its nature, voluntary and often takes the form of neighbourhood care. Since it is voluntary it largely relies upon friendship and *being with* people rather than explicitly *doing things for* them. There is less distinction of roles and functions, more flexibility and possibly more equality in the relationship. As an addition, alongside other services, and often requiring professional support in some way, it is important for professionals to be aware of the potential of this type of resource. There are many such projects and Woods' (1981) description of the PACE group for parents of young handicapped children in Leeds is an excellent example.

The Home-Start voluntary service scheme is another and more comprehensive example of a non-professional support service (Van Der Eyken, 1982). Professional involvement is at the level of steering committees which provide advice and management support and ensure liaison with local services. Funding is essential and comes from varied sources such as Urban Aid, Inner Area Programmes, local authority departments and charities. Home-Start was initiated in Leicester in 1973 and has now developed into a well organized and evaluated service. A Home-Start consultancy has been set up to advise other developments.

Central to the scheme is the use of volunteers and its independence from statutory services. It focuses on families which have young children and which are experiencing frustrations and difficulties. Referrals come from local services, such as health visitors and social workers, and from families themselves. The main aim is to provide a volunteer who can visit the family at home as frequently as desired, sharing their time, concern, optimism and *friendship*, and offering practical help through such activities as playing with the children, talking over problems, providing company, helping in the home, or helping the family to get out. In this way it is hoped to reduce the stresses on the family and help parents to develop new ideas, skills, relationships and confidence in themselves.

The scheme has an organizer responsible for daily management, volunteer selection and support. Volunteers are carefully chosen from a variety of backgrounds and ages. Their attitudes are important and they have often themselves been the recipients of help in the past. They are given a short induction course (for example, one day per week for ten weeks) which covers such areas as the Home-Start approach, basic child development, ethics and skills of visiting, understanding relationships and available community resources. They are then matched to one, two or three families and visit regularly. Volunteers keep brief records of contacts which are totally confidential to the scheme. An essential component, as noted earlier in relation to professional services, is the need to give support to the volunteers. This is provided on an individual basis with the organizer or the referral agent, or in small monthly group meetings.

Home visiting has also been supplemented by weekly group parent meetings of an informal, supportive nature and more educational monthly meetings based on talks and films. Outings, visits and parties are often included, adding a social dimension.

The Leicester Home-Start scheme has been evaluated by Van Der Eyken (1982) who concluded that the scheme was beneficial. Of note was that initially many of the families involved had only a rudimentary support network. The volunteers created a friendship pattern that was often absent and which subsequently developed into a support network and increased parent confidence and competence.

Home–School Links

There are many forms of home–school links and a considerable volume of literature is available (Cyster, Clift & Battle, 1980; Craft,

Raynor & Cohen, 1980). To review these is beyond the scope and intent of this book. Many variations relate to local resources and the type of school. For example, nursery schools have far more access to daily, informal contact as mothers deliver and pick up their children, whilst secondary schools have to establish more formal methods. The same is true for special schools, which are faced with large catchment areas. In those catering for moderate learning difficulties, many children come from lower socio-economic groupings and there may therefore be difficulties with transport, fewer families with telephones, and some who are not experienced in dealing with formal written communications.

Regardless of local variations there are common principles to guide improvement of home–school liaison. Midwinter (1973) argued that this should be seen as a public relations exercise and suggested four phases:

(i) *Publication*: The purpose is to present parents with information on philosophy and aims, activities and how the school functions generally.

(ii) *Exposition*: Opening up the school to public view through easier access and the use of educative and social functions, such as exhibitions, plays and gymnastics, art and craft displays.

(iii) *Site improvements*: Ensuring that the school looks attractive and provides space for parental activities.

(iv) *Involvement*: Involving parents directly in the education process by having parent associations, communal events and home activities in relation to child learning.

These principles are common to any establishment or attempt to work with parents.

Written communications should be attractive, relevant, useful and readable. The function, nature and usefulness of school reports for parents has recently been examined by Goacher & Reid (1984) and their work indicates how styles and attitudes are reflected in the school organization. Schools with successful links usually have well produced prospectuses and regular newsletters. These, together with well presented displays and improvement of the site are important in creating the impression of valuing the children and the work of the school. This is also reflected in demonstrating an understanding of parents' needs. Some schools with large catchment areas provide transport or hold some meetings at more local and convenient venues for parents. Special schools are beginning to set aside a room for parents. These display work and school publications and also provide information on services and books for borrowing. The parents do not have to wait self-consciously in a corridor, but can go directly to the parents' room, thus emphasizing that they are welcomed, which is a major principle noted by the Plowden Report.

Of course, not all families want or can make use of these forms of involvement. Home-visits are indispensible but difficult to organize for all teaching staff. Apart from resource problems, many teachers have reservations about home visits. Thus, the use of Home-Liaison Teachers or, in some schools, an attached social worker, is not uncommon. This has the advantage of opening up a home-to-school information channel, in addition to the more typical school-to-home links. The latter are inevitably one way and controlled by the professional. Non-crisis visits can also be made which, because they are carried out in a relatively stress free context, are more likely to build up positive links. However, a home–school teacher service can only function if the remainder of the staff find their work with the child is enhanced by the service. This requires rapid dissemination of information to staff and a shared set of aims and values between staff.

The involvement of parents in educational activities at home requires careful consideration. Many parents who have experienced early intervention programmes and desire and expect to be involved, look to the school for continuing guidance. Many schools use a home–school diary on a daily, or more often, weekly basis. Activities in school are noted and this provides parents with some idea of things to talk about and areas of interest to extend. These are generally welcomed by parents, especially for children with communication difficulties who are unable to explain what they have been doing. However, maintaining diaries can be time consuming and often can do no more than make general points. They can often break down when parents feel unable to use them or feel they are not meeting their needs. Many parents want more practical and detailed guidance on how to help the child attain new skills and how to maintain and generalize ones learnt at school. This need can be met by parent workshops or groups, or by detailed charts to guide what games to play or how to encourage reading. In time a library of these can be developed to supplement the diaries.

Bland statements of 'listen to him read' are not sufficient and may well cause conflict unless parents and teachers share common methods. The recent series of studies using the Paired Reading approach is a useful example of how parent–professional collaboration can be highly effective when one moves from simple, wishful platitudes to a negotiated approach in which parent, professional and child have respect and control, and quickly master and understand the techniques. Paired reading consists of the child and parent reading together for short 5 to 15 minute sessions on a regular basis. It has two aspects: if the child is not very confident or the reading material is relatively difficult, they both read aloud together with the parent adjusting his/her speed or rhythm to the child's and pointing to the words. If, on the other hand, the child feels confident, he/she can select to read aloud alone by using a pre-negotiated signal. If the child makes a mistake or does not read a word within four or five seconds, the parent reads the word and they continue to read together until the child signals again.

Many of the principles of parent involvement outlined earlier are illustrated in this approach. Firstly, the method is relatively easy to understand and is within the immediate competence of most parents: in fact many intuitively use such methods. Hence, when initially proposed to parents, it does not present itself as requiring complex pre-training which may be threatening to some and emphasize incompetence. Instead, it is an approach that can be relatively quickly put into practice with a high likelihood of success. However, careful planning, demonstration and supervised training of parent and child are required. Particular care must be taken to warn parents that achieving the synchrony of reading together may take some time. They should also realize the importance of avoiding heavy use of correctional procedures which can be frustrating to child and parent, break up the fluency of the reading and can spoil the pleasure of understanding and sharing the meaning of what is being read. Thus, discussion with parents about the rationale of the approach is important.

The aim of Paired Reading is to develop fluency and understanding. It is a complementary activity to reading instruction in schools and not an attempt to extend or transplant the classroom/teacher method into the home. This recognizes the distinction between parent and teacher roles and the parent–child relationship. Without guidance, parents have to rely on their past experience or available information, in this case books about reading are often aimed at professionals. It is not surprising that this often leads to unhappy experiences for the child and parent, especially if the parent construes the teaching role as highly didactic. In Paired Reading, if the child makes a mistake or fails to read the word within four or five seconds, the parent does not comment or draw attention to the failure by explaining how the word is made up, and so breaking the fluency, but instead provides a good model of the word which the child then repeats and they continue reading.

Another important feature of the approach is the respect for the child. The child selects the reading material regardless of difficulty and also has shared control (and therefore responsibility) of reading alone, using the signal to stop the parent reading aloud. This also respects the difference between the parent–child relationship discussed in previous chapters. Of course no one method suits all parents or children and adaptations are needed or alternatives. Even so, the initial evaluations of this approach are encouraging and it clearly offers a tangible approach for the development of parent–teacher partnerships.

Similarly, many parents would like to take a direct part in recreational and educational activities within the school, though this can result in conflict unless careful preparation is made and values and aims are shared. Again, some schools have found that having a parent base in the school and parent group activities can gradually lead to a shared philosophy of roles from which voluntary use of parents for small groups or individual activities arises.

Exchange of information is also part of the accountability exercise. By definition, to be accountable is to recognize responsibility, and the exercise is to demonstrate that one is meeting these responsibilities. This only happens if the objectives are demonstrable and appropriate measures are available. If accountability is going to be meaningful exercise, then the person to whom one is accounting has to feel that the objectives are valid. Thus in accounting to be a meaningful exercise, then the person to whom one is accounting has to feel that the objectives are valid. Thus in accounting to parents, the exercise will not be useful unless they share the same appreciation of the judgements (values and expectations) report card demonstrating progress in curriculum areas may fail, if the parent does not share the importance of the objectives. Indeed, unless parents have been prepared in advance and some joint agreement or objective has been reached, the information exchange may result in conflict. Equally, the parent has to believe that the measures used to arrive at an assessment of the child are reliable and valid.

Unless this first step of arriving at jointly agreed goals and approaches is met, then there is an increased likelihood of conflict. Since accountability to parents, and in the case of working partnerships, parents to professionals, is rapidly expanding, those who fail to realize this first step and merely report results may find themselves in conflict. This produces stress and anxiety, which can then lead to avoidance behaviour such as reduced interaction between partners or denial of responsibility, with the partners blaming each other. Such blame often includes pathological constructs like 'they don't care', 'they abdicate their responsibilities' or 'they are too stupid to understand'. All these have been aimed at parents by professionals and at professionals by parents. However, while many schools have policies about parent involvement, few actually attempt systematically to evaluate this by asking parents. Since, as we stated in Chapter 1, it is important to listen to parents, this has obviously been seriously neglected here.

Most successful home–school links find that parent involvement takes time and is a gradual process. Many considerations have to be taken into account and should be planned as a series of small, progressive innovations, each being evaluated and consolidated in the daily school routines before the next is attempted. As in any programme of change, success brings increased confidence and willingness to progress. Failure can inhibit change and establish negative constructions which are likely to lead to self-fulfilling prophecies.

Conclusions and Issues

All the approaches that we have described in this chapter attempt to help children with special needs and their families. Some focus more upon the child, seeing the parent as a means of facilitating his/her development. By doing so, there is a greater possibility of implicitly adopting a transplant model. Those which focus primarily upon the parent, or family as a whole, and are concerned to strengthen the resources and relationships within the family, appear much more likely to adopt a consumer/partnership model.

Most, despite their original perspective, generally find a need to broaden their programme and encompass wider issues. Approaches intended to explore emotional and adjustment difficulties, find the provision of practical help and skill training useful. Conversely, those intended to provide skill training have to explore adjustment difficulties. Home-based approaches find the need to extend parent social interactions and to provide access to groups, whilst centre-based approaches have to include some element of home and individual based consultation.

That parents benefit considerably from talking to other parents and non-professionals is almost universally noted. The support gained from these sources appears to be particularly related to reducing stress, fostering parental growth and development and, through this, the child's well–being.

How this actually happens is not well understood. What

emerges from the review is that non-professional interaction can offer a different and unique type of support. Throughout the book we have discussed how the professional can enter into a mutually respectful, open partnership based on the sharing of knowledge, information, resources, power and decision-making. This is a partnership of equality, but it is the differences the two partners bring to the collaboration that is important. The professional is expected to have specialized competence and, at least partially, to be able to solve problems. This is not, however, friendship. We would suggest that the professional has to be seen by the parent as someone who has competence and is helpful. In order to do this, we believe the professional has to maintain some emotional distance which enables him/her to stand back and look in a more dispassionate way. This not only helps the professional to function more effectively and add to the partnership, it may also prevent the professional from being overwhelmed by the problems. This does, however, highlight the fact that the relationship between the parent and professional is obviously different from the relationship between a parent and other parents or, as in the Home-Start example, a parent and volunteer.

Essentially, parents get together to be with each other and to give and to receive support and to share experiences. They are parents, however, with the characteristics described in Chapter 2, having diffuse roles, high attachment, more spontaneity in comparison with the professional and so on. The relationship with a professional is expected to be more intentional or goal directed, objective and specific to their area of specialism. Consequently, parents will not construe other parents or volunteers in the same way as they construe the professional. They are less likely to expect and direct their energy to specific areas, as they might with the professional, and are more likely to explore in a broader and freer way a range of feelings and topics. The nature of the discourse will therefore be different. They may, for example, be more willing to return to the same ideas over and over and to listen to or relate a wider range of anecdotes. When alternative suggestions are given, they may be more willing to consider them critically, neither assuming that they are correct because they are given by a person construed as an expert, nor with suspicion of the hidden agendas held by the professional.

Partly because of this, parents may be more able to compare their constructions with other parents and therefore be more able to reformulate their construct system in the comparative safety of shared identity. Since it may be that the majority of people change their views of the world through discourse as opposed to the more academic modes of lectures and books, it could be that parent–parent interactions are more natural. They may offer more acceptable and enjoyable repetition to consolidate the reconstruction process. Hence, in working with parents, professionals may need to give far more attention to social support networks and informal interactions than is currently apparent.

This is not an argument for the unimportance of professional services, but for a clearer appreciation of different functions. For example, another consistent finding from most of the work with parents is that, while they may not maintain the same levels of structured teaching in their involvement with the child once programmes have finished, they do appear to fit their new learning into their own routines and become more confident and, in turn, more opportunistic and spontaneous. However, where there is continuing learning difficulties with the child, then the parents do require access to continual support and they do desire information on activities to help the child. This must be provided by competent professionals who can develop programmes and advise on methods.

In this context, another issue yet to be resolved, is the extent to which the parent should or can function in a didactic teaching role with the child. This may not be possible for many parents and children because of their special relationship. As noted in Chapter 2, the parents' constructions of the child and their interactions with the child are different from that of the professional because they are the parent. Similarly, the child's constructions of what the parent does and what this means cannot be the same as the child's constructions of the professional's actions. Thus the child may interpret parents who are acting consistently and intentionally in a corrective fashion as cold, angry or displeased, whereas they would construe the same behaviour in the teacher as normal and appropriate. Merely transplanting professional methods into parents without considering their wider context may interfere with the relationship and it is not surprising that many parents say they cannot comply with professional advice.

The extent to which parents can adopt more formal teaching approaches will also vary according to the child's development level. In late infancy and the pre-school period, children generally are less willing to engage in formal teaching sessions than the more compliant early infancy stage or later childhood. Thus the more formal techniques of highly structured teaching are often less easy to apply to many children at this stage. 'I tried it like you suggested, but we both got angry and fed up. So I've just made it part of a game.'

It is also suggested that if the parent adopts an extreme didactic teaching style, this may fail to develop feelings of self-efficacy in the child and may merely condition a highly dependent relationship. In other words, just as there is a suggestion that the professional–parent relationship can create dependency, so the same concerns can be applied to the relationship between the parent and child.

Traditionally, developmental delay is diagnosed in the child by comparing what he/she can do on developmental tests with the standardized norms. Many programmes, like Portage, use the activities of such tests as the content of their teaching with the intention of enabling children to match the normal performance at as early an age as possible. This approach, therefore, focuses upon the child's relative weaknesses and in this sense emphasizes more pathological aspects such as sensory, physical or learning deficits, a lack of self initiation, and an inability to formulate conceptions or to construe: hence the stereotype of these children as passive recipients of external events may be reinforced. Construed in this way the children are seen as mainly requiring highly structured teaching approaches in order to compensate for their learning difficulties, as in the use of behavioural techniques.

However, from an alternative viewpoint, one can see the child as an active construer, seeking to make sense of events. This is close to cognitive models that see child development as the sequential formation of internal representations which the child uses selectively on his/her environment. The child is seen as an active participant who demands some control over her/his interactions.

Models such as these have led to early intervention programmes which train parents more in the ability to develop and maintain relationships and interactions with the child and to set up learning situations which encourage self-exploration and regulation (Affleck, *et al.*, 1982; Bromwich, 1981; Fraiberg, 1977). Such programmes do not deny the child's difficulty, but construe him/her differently. Consequently, they overtly or covertly convey a different set of constructs to the parents about the handicap, and therefore, about the child. This may have major implications for their relationship, aspirations and actions in relation to the child in the long term.

Again, we see that the explicit or implicit models that people have to control their actions require careful examination. The above brief comparison is meant to exemplify this, rather than to suggest that one model is always more appropriate than another. In reality some aspects of development in some children may be better served by one model than another. Given the lack of well evaluated comparative studies, most professionals must currently be open-minded and eclectic.

Practical Exercise

Individual schools or units differ considerably in the extent to which they actively seek to involve parents. To help decide to what degree and how parents are involved in a particular setting, it may be useful to carry out the following exercise. The answers should help you decide whether the school has considered these matters at both a policy level and a practical level and the extent to which parents have been involved in planning, decision-making and evaluation.

Take a school in which you work or which you know well and answer the questions listed below. If you are not familiar yourself with a school then try to interview a friend, colleague or parent who is well acquainted with a school and ask them the questions.

1. Does the school have an explicit policy about contacting/meeting parents?
2. If so, what is it?
3. Is there a clear, written statement of the policy available to staff and parents?
4. Are parent involvement procedures arrived at by joint parent–teacher consensus?
5. Is there flexibility in the ways of involving parents?
6. Is parent involvement largely problem-orientated?
7. Is there a system for recording parent contacts?
8. Is there a method for evaluating parent reactions to school involvement methods?
9. Is time made available for staff to meet and talk to parents?
10. Is information routinely provided for parents?
11. Do parents have opportunities to meet and talk to each other at school?
12. Is there a base set aside for parents in the school?
13. Are parents seen as individuals and given individual attention?
14. Do staff and parents interact in ways that indicate mutual respect and equality as opposed to an inferior-superior relationship created by the idea of the 'expert'?
15. Is information provided for parents to help them evaluate:
    (i) the school attainments generally
    (ii) their own child's attainments

16. Does the school project a welcoming, valuing image for child and parent?
17. Are school records on families open to parent inspection?

CHAPTER 8

Final Remarks

In a previously happy family of three children, the involvement of the middle girl in a serious traffic accident when she was seven years old was a massive shock. She survived and recovered in health, but serious head injuries left her with speech and movement difficulties. Although not extreme, she also showed some behaviour problems in that her sleep patterns were altered and she was socially withdrawn.

When she was discharged from hospital, she was referred for physiotherapy and speech therapy and was also seen by a clinical psychologist. This meant that the family had to visit the hospital (a 45 minute drive from their home) twice a week on average. The parents were also required to spend about an hour a day carrying out various phsyiotherapy and speech therapy exercises at home, as well as conducting a programme to establish an acceptable sleep routine and making observations on other aspects of the child's behaviour.

Although the various departments were in the same hospital, there was apparently no co-ordination of their activities until a liaison social worker was appointed to the family. Unfortunately, for various reasons, mainly organizational, she did not meet the family until two months or so after discharge. In the meantime the therapists noticed that the family began to complain about the hospital and to miss appointments. As a result they were labelled as unco-operative, and interaction with them became somewhat brittle. In turn they complained more frequently and missed more appointments.

Eventually the social worker visited the family at home to explore their situation with them. In particular she saw her role

155

as firstly identifying the stresses on the family and their resources
and secondly as helping the family to formulate treatment goals.
She found a series of very obvious sources of stress. The first
was the lack of time. The child's treatment and visits to the hospital
took so much time that the mother felt the housework suffered;
both parents said there was no time for the other children, and
they no longer did things as a family. The second source was
the demands of the home treatment routines. The parents felt
that the three different therapists had given them conflicting
advice, though they admitted being unable to understand and
assimilate all the instructions. They wanted to do everything they
could to treat their daughter, yet felt unable to meet the treatment
demands. They became highly uncertain about what they were
doing and not confident in their ability to benefit her. They
expressed considerable dissatisfaction with themselves and the
services, and showed a general loss of compliance.

The third source of stress was financial. There was the cost
of travel to the hospital; the mother needed the car to take her
daughter, and so the father had to use public transport and therefore took longer to travel to and from work. He also had to take
time off and lost overtime. Mother gave up her part-time job and
yet they had to pay for changes to their house to accommodate
the child's physical problems. As the mother said;

> 'We don't seem to get time to do anything since the accident. I
> am always having to catch up with the housework and laundry.
> He (the father) had to service the car last weekend, because we've
> got to save money . . . Things just seem to be getting out of control
> and I don't know what to do for the best. I think she has improved
> a little but I don't know if it's because of all the effort . . . My husband
> thinks we're wasting our time'.

With the social worker's help, the family decided on a plan
of action to reduce the stresses. The social worker liaised with
other people treating the child and set up a 'team' to work out
a rational plan for the family as a whole as opposed to three separate plans all focused solely on the child. Not all the difficulties
were solved, but a balance was achieved in negotiation with the
family. The parents learned mechanisms for testing and expressing feelings, and they provided feedback to the professional team
via the social worker. The team achieved a better perspective of
the family needs and also managed to reduce the total amount
of professional time allotted to the family by avoiding duplicity
of action. Both the professionals and the family felt happier about
the situation.

Most importantly, as the family began to feel in control of their lives again, they were able to reorganize their routines and even to organize help from relatives and friends, which further reduced their demands on the services. Financial problems were eased and the parents felt confident that these would be resolved once they became aware of their rights to state support (e.g. Attendance Allowance).

Although this final example highlights the frameworks and skills described in the book, it also raises many issues that have had to be left out. What we would like to do here, therefore, is to draw out some of these issues for consideration.

1. Service Organization

The first issue is the need for service organization and co-ordination. The example shows that no matter how skilled individual professionals become, their help may be severely limited, and even destructive, if they work in isolation, unaware of what other professionals are doing. At the very least it is important for each professional to make an assessment and, of course, to negotiate the extent to which the family can be expected to participate actively.

As has been emphasized in recent years, there is a need for professionals to work together in teams (Simon, 1981). The Court Report recommended in 1976 the establishment of multidisciplinary teams to provide diagnostic/assessment and treatment/educational services for children with handicaps. It was suggested that these should consist of a paediatrician, nursing officer, social worker, psychologist and teacher. As a result by 1981, 25 per cent of health districts had set up what are called District Handicap Teams or Child Development Teams. For the mentally handicapped as a whole, Community Mental Handicap Teams are being set up.

Nevertheless, simply establishing such teams can only be effective if all professions are prepared to work closely with all others. Just as there has been a tendency to deny parents a role in helping the child, so professionals often display a tendency to defend their vested interests and to deny or devalue the roles of others. Naturally, such interdisciplinary rivalry does not foster good working relationships, good communication or effective team functioning. Further problems in the establishment of adequate co-ordinated

facilities are the administrative boundaries between health, education and social services. Power struggles about such boundaries
can hinder efforts to benefit those who are supposedly being
served.

For teams to function effectively, we would argue that many
of the attributes of counsellors and the models discussed in previous chapters are appropriate. For example, the way that professionals construe each other will affect their interaction, as will
the skills they have for communicating. What is necessary is for
team members to respect each other and to establish good relationships in order to negotiate mutually acceptable goals and actions;
they should work in partnership. In principle such partnerships
should be the same as with parents. A prerequisite is that each
member of the team brings his/her own expertise and complementary skills and has equal status. This would be enhanced if they
all shared a set of counselling skills, which were acknowledged
to be essential aspects of their professional role.

The term 'multidisciplinary' to describe such teams, implies that
the child, and perhaps the family, are treated by several specialists
from different backgrounds using different theoretical models. The
danger is that each specialist may have a restricted view of a given
problem and will contribute strictly limited data. They may also
communicate by written report only, using specialized jargon.
In this situation which profession is competent to put the various
information together into a whole? Certain information may also
be missed, in particular the psychological functioning of the
family.

A better term than 'multidisciplinary' is perhaps 'interdisciplinary' since it implies specialists working more closely together. In
this situation the success of the team will be partly due to attributes such as respect and communication, and also due to training
together over a number of years. By sharing specialist knowledge,
to some extent the professionals must acquire skills enabling them
to function across disciplines. With this as an ideal, it is even
more appropriate to use the term 'transdisciplinary'.

This does not mean that each professional may make an in-depth
medical examination or be able to teach children skilfully. It does
imply, however, that each professional should be able to take
responsibility for co-ordinating information about any particular
family in order to make the most effective decisions in negotiating
with them. This becomes particularly possible if professionals all
share the kind of core skills with which we have been concerned.
When any member of any profession can say they know all the
answers to the problems of special needs, only then can they

work alone or dominate other professions. Though equality of status may be assumed, this does not deny that a team must be organized and led by a competent chairperson and deputy who may be elected or appointed on some kind of rotational system.

2. Support for the Professional

A second issue to be raised is the need for individual professionals to be supported in their work. This is particularly true when the professional has a very heavy workload and is working with chronic problems and in extreme social circumstances, where success may not be obvious or dramatic. When working closely in partnership with parents, it may be that professionals are even more vulnerable to stresses; they are, as we have said, more open to scrutiny and have to work with parents who may not be as 'reasonable' as other professionals. If they adopt a partnership model and widen their perspective to encompass the family and community, they will meet more uncertainty, and they will be less able to protect themselves behind their professional expertise and limited area of responsibility. In such situations the professional may easily become disillusioned, demoralized and discouraged.

One of the functions of a professional team, therefore, apart from the more obvious administrative, assessment and treatment/ educational functions, is to provide support for its members. Team meetings may be arranged where all members can share and discuss their feelings, problems, successes and failures. Like any parent support group, the success of such meetings will depend upon the mutual agreement of the members about the purpose and format of the meeting, and again, the need for respectful and trusting relationships is clear, otherwise the situation may be one of threat as opposed to support. Such support needs as careful planning as does that which professionals provide for parents. Thus, the counselling framework and skills discussed in Chapter 6, Personal Construct Theory in Chapters 3 and 4, and aspects of stress and social networks described in Chapter 5 are as relevant here as they are for working with parents and families.

3. Family Focused Service

The case at the beginning of the chapter highlighted the tendency for many services to remain very much child focused. The personnel (e.g. paediatrician, occupational therapist, or teacher) are child oriented in training and in their job specification. Relatively few, for example, are given time to work with the family as a whole, though a major issue is, of course, the extent to which different professions should be involved in counselling or family concerns if they have not been trained to do so. Other professions, like social workers, are more family orientated, but their time is severely limited. The professions working in the area of child psychiatry emphasize a family approach, though they tend to work only with emotional problems and are relatively rarely involved in handicap or educational problems.

Given such circumstances of child orientated job specification, poor resources, lack of training in working with families and relatively little professional training in psychological skills generally, it is not surprising to find generalized neglect of family problems as a whole, except when they have become so gross as to be obvious. Even when identified, there remains a general feeling of inadequacy and helplessness with respect to what can be done.

The needs can be demonstrated and yet educational and medical services are in general not psychologically or socially orientated, and academic achievement and physical care are still the main priority. Thus medical staff will argue that psychological wellbeing is low in priority, when adequate health care services have not yet been achieved. This difficulty reflects the fact that each discipline has its own set of priorities and there appears to be no professional discipline that has as its main priority the psychosocial aspects of the individual and family. Consequently, any current multidisciplinary team will have to develop this area.

This, of course, raises the issue of policy decisions at all levels of the services. The need for consideration of the psychological wellbeing of individuals has implications at a national level in terms of resource provision and training of professionals. At another level, each school or hospital or even class or ward must formulate policies on, for example, what information is to be communicated to parents, by whom, when and how.

To remedy the situation resources are also needed. One can employ specialists such as psychiatrists, psychologists, social workers or home liaison teachers with a brief to be family orientated. Even so, it is difficult to envisage this meeting the demand. An alternative is to train all those currently working in the area of special needs and to allow time for them to consider families as a whole. Again, this implies the need for a transdisciplinary approach in which professional barriers and territoriality are broken down, and skills and knowledge shared.

4. Voluntary Bodies

Given deficits in service resources another issue to be considered is the role of the voluntary bodies. Although various organizations such as Mencap, Down's Syndrome Association and the Spastics Society have been in existence for a long time, it is apparent that their relationship with official services is far from clear. Although some professionals work closely with these bodies, many ignore them and others are somewhat threatened by them. This may be partly because they act as pressure groups for service reform, but also because the barrier between professional and parent is somewhat eroded by organizations that largely consist of parents.

Since the voluntary bodies are an enormous potential source of resource and expertise, it is important that close links be fostered between paid professionals and the volunteers. Such links are very much in line with the notions of partnership discussed in Chapter 2. It is clear that these organizations can add to, complement and make up for the deficiencies in functions that may currently be seen as the province of the professional. Examples of this were provided in Chapter 7. By their very existence voluntary bodies may provide generalized support through the communication of relevant information by newsletters and other publications. They can also extend the social support network of families and reduce social isolation as in the case of Mencap's Gateway movement. There are examples of parent–parent support schemes in various parts of the country, and it is possible for them to provide more elaborately trained counsellors as evidenced for example by the Marriage Guidance Association.

5. Alternative Ways of Helping

Since the area of special needs is so diverse, no perfect system has yet been devised to remedy all the problems. There is the constant need to explore new ideas and evolving technology. A major need for families and professionals is quick access to up-to-date and accurate information. In many circumstances this is done most effectively on a one-to-one counselling basis. In other cases, and if resources are short, less costly alternatives such as pamphlets, books, workshops and group approaches are useful. However, as discussed in the last chapter, not all people can derive benefits from books or lectures and other approaches need to be explored.

Such sources of information may, to speculate, become much more efficiently provided through the use of microcomputers. It is not impossible to conceive of the provision of large databases of information about types, causes and remedies of special needs and the resources available. For example, this service could be provided by public libraries in the form of floppy discs to be borrowed, or even accessed via telephone links. This would capitalize on the increasing availability of microcomputers in homes and offices.

Of course, books and computers require a somewhat academic approach in the sense of the inclination to read extensively, and they are restricted to certain types of information. As such this may be less available to some parents than other possibilities. Wider use could be made of the proliferation of home-video machines. Video-recordings are increasingly being made for parent and professional training. Currently this is usually in the context of a professionally controlled training course. However, it is foreseeable that video programmes, again accessible via a public library, could be made to inform and instruct parents about all aspects of special needs.

Although these methods of information dissemination do not dispense with professional services, they do have the possible advantage of being controlled by parents themselves. Consequently, the issue of the development of self-confidence and self-competence that we have stressed as an aim of counselling may be served to a large extent by these methods in a way that reduces pressures upon professionals directly. On the other hand, the need for detailed evaluation of consumer needs becomes more obvious in such schemes, as they have to meet a large range of individual differences using the same format.

6. A Positive Approach

A final issue we wish to raise is the need to adopt a positive approach in any services provided. We have discussed the tendency to use pathological models in relation to both children with special needs and their parents. Characteristically, such models focus upon weaknesses or problems, as opposed to strengths, and they fail to provide ways of viewing situations that imply the possibility of remedial action; they are self-defeating in implication.

What is important is to find models that are positive in suggesting avenues to explore. The underlying analogy of Personal Construct Theory (Chapter 3) is 'man the scientist', and this is one of the reasons for suggesting it so strongly. There is not one way of explaining events, but many alternative ways, all of which are hypotheses to be tested by our actions as a result. Children are not 'ineducable' or 'unhelpable' by definition whatever their special needs. No matter how severe their impairments there are positive courses of action. They can be positively viewed as children with families, all members of which may be helped to make the most appropriate level of adjustment within their particular circumstances. Such adjustment can be construed as helpful for the child in that it enhances his/her quality of life through the interactions with family members.

The analogy with science has the implication of generating hypotheses and ideas, looking at events and situations from all points of view and exploring and testing them for their usefulness, thereby gaining a better understanding. The stance adopted by the scientist is one of scepticism, not taking anything at face value without careful evaluation. As such, therefore, it may be argued that the approach in itself is one of uncertainty which has the disadvantage of further increasing the parents' and professionals' lack of knowledge and acceptance. On the other hand, it is possible to see this uncertainty positively, since although it does not specify the end point or final conclusion to be reached, it does give direction.

It directs by implying exploration of alternatives. It allows movement and change, where both professional and parent may be stuck. It allows the possibility of useful conclusions and actions being explored with potential benefit, even though it does not provide the destination at the outset. For example, it may be of value to parents, when they do not know whether or when their child will walk or talk, to view themselves as engaged in the process of exploration of possibilities. It is a positive model of both themselves and their child, even though uncertainty surrounds them.

The value of this approach may be further exemplified, since the professional may frequently be in a position of not knowing what to do. In a family with multiple problems, it is never obvious where to start in tackling them. Does one begin, for example, with the child's behaviour problems, or with educational deficits; with the mother's or father's negative self-images or their failing marriage? Construing the professional's intervention with the family as an experiment goes some way to resolving such situations. It implies making the best guess possible at the time (the hypothesis), deciding goals and actions on the basis of the guess (the experiment) and carefully evaluating the outcome (the results). This process, if nothing else, in itself provides information to increase understanding of the situation, but it also sets the family in motion. They may change and by changing, know they can change.

As discussed in Chapter 5, family systems are complex with changes at one point having ramifications throughout. As such, because of the complexity, there is no way of predicting outcome with any great certainty, so that provoking change is perhaps the best that can be done.

It is interesting to note in this connection that evidence suggests that one does not have to deal with all of a family's problems. It is often the case that a beneficial change in one aspect (e.g. the marital relationship or the child's behavioural disturbance) will be associated with many other subsequent changes. There is, of course, the possibility of producing negative change inadvertently, but if one only acted when absolutely certain of the outcome, then no professional intervention could be undertaken; lack of knowledge would prohibit action entirely. It is perhaps a reality, therefore, to say that all the professional can hope to do is to help the family to change, with the direction subsequently determined largely by the family.

Similarly, we cannot know what ultimate conclusions the reader will have reached by reading this book. Even with an absolute knowledge of the reader's characteristics it would be impossible to say. What we hope, however, is to have provoked change. If we have made you reconsider your assumptions, made you think about your practices from alternative viewpoints, then we have set a process in motion that allows the possibility of developments to occur without specifying an outcome, which is more in the readers' control than our own.

References

Abidin, R. (1980). *Parent Education and Intervention Handbook*. Springfield, Thomas.

Affleck, G., McGrade, B., McQueeney, M. & Allen, D. (1982). 'Relationship-focussed early intervention in developmental disabilities'. *Exceptional Child*, 49, 259–261.

Aplin, G. & Pugh, G. (1983). *Perspectives on Pre-School Home Visiting*. London, National Childrens Bureau.

Bannister, D. and Fransella, F. (1980). *Inquiring Man*. Harmondsworth, Penguin.

Beail, N. & McGuire, J. (1982). *Psychological Aspects of Fatherhood*. London, Junction.

Berger, E. (1981). *Parents as Partners in Education*. St. Louis, Mosby.

Blacher, J. (1984). *Severely Handicapped Young Children and Their Families: Research in Review*. London, Academic Press.

Bromwich, R. (1981). *Working with Parents and Infants: an Interactional Approach*. Baltimore, University Park Press.

Bowlby, J. (1951). *Maternal Care and Mental Health*. Geneva, W.H.O.

Burden, R. (1980). 'Measuring the effects of stress on the mothers of handicapped infants: must depression always follow?'. *Child: Care, Health and Development*, 6, 111–125.

Burgoyne, L. & Clarke, A. (1984). *Making a Go of it*. London, Routledge & Kegan Paul.

Cameron, R.J. (1982). *Working Together: Portage in the U.K.* Windsor, NFER-Nelson.

Carr, J (1980). *Helping Your Handicapped Child*. Harmondsworth, Penguin.

Carter, P. & McGoldrick, N. (1980). *The Family Life Cycle: A Framework for Family Therapy*. New York, Gardner Press.

Craft, M., Raynor, J. & Cohen, L. (1980). *Linking Home and School: A New Review*. London, Harper and Row.

Cunningham, C.C. & Jeffree, D. (1975). 'Organisation and structure of workshops for parents of mentally handicapped children.' *Bulletin of the British Psychological Society*, 28, 405–411.

Cunningham, C.C. & Sloper, P. (1978). *Helping Your Handicapped Baby.* London, Souvenir Press.

Cyster, R., Clift, P.S. & Battle, S. (1980). *Parent Involvement In Schools.* Slough, NFER.

Davis, H. and Cunningham, C. (1985). 'Mental handicap'. In E. Button (ed.) *Personal Construct Theory and Mental Health.* London, Croom Helm.

De Meyers, M. (1979). *Parents and Children in Autism.* London, Wiley.

Dessent, T. (1984). *What is Important About Portage?* Windsor, NFER-Nelson.

Diamond, S. (1981). 'Growing up with parents of a handicapped child'. In J. Paul (ed.) *Understanding & Working with Parents of Children with Special Needs.* New York, Holt, Rinehart & Winston.

Egan, G. (1981). *The Skilled Helper.* Monterey, Brooks/cole.

Featherstone, H. (1981). *A Difference in the Family: Living with a Disabled Child.* Harmondsworth, Penguin.

Firth, H. (1982). 'The effectiveness of parent workshops in a mental handicap service'. *Child: Care, Health and Development,* 8, 77–91.

Folkman, S., Schaffer, C. & Lazarus, R. (1979). 'Cognitive processes as mediators of stress and coping'. In V. Hamilton & D. Warburton (eds.) *Human Stress and Cognition.* New York, Wiley.

Fraiberg, S. (1977). *Insights from the Blind.* London, Souvenir Press.

Friedrich, W. & Friedrich, W. (1981). Psychosocial aspects of parents of handicapped and non-handicapped children'. *American Journal of Mental Deficiency,* 85, 551–553.

Freud, S. (1974). *Introductory Lectures on Psychoanalysis.* Harmondsworth, Penguin.

Gath, A. (1978). *Down's Syndrome and the Family: The Early Years.* London, Academic Press.

Glendinning, C. (1983). *Parents and their Disabled Children.* London, Routledge & Kegan Paul.

Goacher, B. & Reid, M. (1984). *School Reports to Parents.* Windsor, NFER-Nelson.

Gottlieb, B.H (1981). *Social Networks And Social Support.* Beverley Hills, Sage.

Gottfried, A. (1984). *Home Environment and Early Cognitive Development.* London, Academic Press.

Gray, S. & Wandersman, I. (1980). 'The methodology of home-based intervention studies: problems and promising strategies.' *Child Development,* 51, 993–1009.

Gregory, S. (1976). *The Deaf Child and his Family.* London, Allen & Unwin.

Hannam, C. (1980). *Parents and Mentally Handicapped Children.* Harmondsworth, Penguin.

Harris, S. (1983). *Families of the Developmentally Disabled: a Guide to Behavioural Intervention.* New York, Pergamon Press.

Heifetz, L. (1980). 'From consumer to middleman: emerging roles for parents in the network of services for retarded children'. In R. Abidin (ed.) *Parent Education and Intervention Handbook.* Springfield, Thomas.

Hewett, S. (1970). *The Family and the Handicapped Child.* London, Allen & Unwin.

Hornby, G. & Singh, N. (1983). 'Group training for parents of mentally retarded children: a review and methodological analysis of behavioural studies.' *Child: Care, Health and Development*, 9, 199–213.

Katz, L. (1980). 'Mothering and teaching: some significant distinctions.' *Current Topics in Early Childhood Education*, 111, 47–63.

Kazak, A. & Marvin, R. (1984). 'Differences, difficulties and adaptation: stress and social networks in families with a handicapped child.' *Family Relations*, 33, 67–77.

Kelly, G.A. (1955). *The Psychology of Personal Constructs*. New York, Norton.

Key, J., Hooper, J & Ballard, M. (1979). 'A parental perspective on the Honeylands Home Visting Project provided by three mothers of older children.' *Child: Care, Health & Development*, 5, 102–109.

Kew, S. (1975). *Handicap and Family Crisis*. London, Pitman.

Lazar, I. & Darlington, R.B. (1982). 'Lasting effects of early education: a report from the consortium for longitudinal studies.' *Monographs of the Society for Research in Child Development*, No. 195, 47 (2–3).

Ley, P. (1982). 'Satisfaction, compliance and communication.' *British Journal of Clinical Psychology*, 21, 241–254.

Lobato, D. (1983). 'Siblings of handicapped children: a review.' *Journal of Autism and Developmental Disorders*, 13, 347–364.

Mackeith, R. (1973). 'The feelings and behaviour of parents of handicapped children.' *Developmental Medicine & Child Neurology*, 15, 24–27.

Marion, R.L. (1981). *Educators, Parents and Exceptional Children*. Rockville, Aspen.

McConachie, H. (1982). 'Fathers of mentally handicapped children.' In N. Beail & J. McGuire (eds.) *Psychological Aspects of Fatherhood*. London, Junction.

McCoy, M. (1977). 'A reconstruction of emotion.' In D. Bannister (ed.) *New Perspectives in Personal Construct Theory*. London, Acadcemic Press.

McConkey, R. & McEvoy, J. (1984). 'Parental Involvement Courses: contrasts between mothers who enrol and those who do not.' In J. Berg (ed.) *Perspectives and Progress in Mental Retardation*. Vol. 1. Baltimore, University Park Press.

Midwinter, E. (1973). *Patterns of Community Education*. London, Ward Lock.

Midwinter, E. (1977). *Education for Sale*. London, Allen & Unwin.

Miezio, P. (1983) *Parenting Children with Disabilities*. New York, Marcel Dekker.

Mink, I., Nihira, K. & Meyes, C. (1983). 'Taxonomy of family life styles: I. Homes with TMR children.' *American Journal of Mental Deficiency*, 87, 484–497

Mittler, P. & McConachie, H. (1983). *Parents, Professionals and Mentally Handicapped People*. London, Croom Helm.

Mittler, P. & Mittler, H. (1982). *Partnership with Parents*. Stratford-upon-Avon, National Council for Special Education.

Murray, M. (1959). 'Needs of parents of mentally handicapped children.' *American Journal of Mental Deficiency*, 632, 1078–1088.

Nelson-Jones, R. (1983). *Practical Counselling Skills*. London, Holt, Rinehart & Winston.

Newson, E. & Hipgrave, T. (1982). *Getting Through to Your Handicapped*

Child. Cambridge, Cambridge University Press.

Newson, J. and Newson, E. (1976). *Seven Year Olds in the Home Environment*. London, Halsted Press.

O'Dell, S. (1974). 'Training parents in behaviour modification: a review.' *Psychological Bulletin*, 81, 418–433.

Olson, D. & McCussin, H. (1983). *Families: What Makes Them Work*. London, Sage.

Paul, J.L. (1981). *Understanding and Working with Parents of Children with Special Needs*. New York, Holt, Rinehart and Winston.

Pope, M. & Keen, T. (1981). *Personal Construct Psychology and Education*, London, Academic Press.

Pugh, G. (1982). *Parents as Partners*. London, National Childrens Bureau.

Raven, J. (1980). *Parents, Teachers and Children: A Study of an Educational Home Visiting Scheme*. Sevenoaks, Hodder & Stoughton.

Rayner, H. (1978). 'The Exeter home-visiting project: the psychologist as one of several therapists.' *Child: Care, Health and Development*, 4, 1–7.

Revill, S. & Blunden, R. (1979). 'A home-training service for pre-school developmentally handicapped children.' *Behaviour, Research and Therapy*, 17, 207–214.

Rotter, J., Chance, J. & Phares, E. (1972). *Applications of a Social Learning Theory of Personality*. New York, Holt, Rinehart & Winston.

Rubissow, J. (1976). 'Honeylands: a family help unit in Exeter.' In Early Management of Handicapped Disorders. *IRMMH Review of Research and Practice*, No. 19, London, IRMMH.

Rutter, M. (1972). *Maternal Deprivation Reassessed*. Harmondsworth, Penguin.

Seligman, M. (1979). *Strategies for Helping Parents of Exceptional Children: A Guide for Teachers*. New York, The Free Press.

Seligman, M. (1982). *Group Psychotherapy and Counselling with Special Populations*. Baltimore, University Park Press.

Seligman, M. (1983). *The Family with a Handicapped Child: Understanding and Treatment*. New York, Grune and Stratton.

Simeonsson, R. & McHale, S. (1981). 'Review: research on handicapped children: sibling relationships.' *Child: Care, Health & Development*, 7, 153–171.

Simon, G.B. (1981). *Local Services for Mentally Handicapped People*. Kidderminster, BIMH.

Slaughter, D.T. (1983). 'Early intervention and its effects on maternal and child development.' *Monograph of the Society for Research in Child Development*, No. 202, 48, (4).

Sloper, P., Cunningham, C.C. & Arnjlsdottir, M. (1983). 'Parental reactions to early intervention.' *Child: Care, Health and Development*, 9, 357–376.

The Consortium for Longitudinal Studies (1983). *As the Turig is Bent . . . Lasting Effects of Preschool Programs*. New Jersey, Lawrence Erlbaum Associates.

Topping, K. & McNight, G. (1984). 'Paired reading and parent power'. *Special Education: Forward Trends*, 11, 12–13.

Van Der Eyken, W. (1982). *Home-Start: A Four Year Evaluation*. Leicester,

Home-Start Consultancy.

Walrond-Skinner, S. (1981). *Developments in Family Therapy*. London, Routledge & Kegan Paul.

Webster, E. (1977). *Counselling with Parents of Handicapped Children*. New York, Grune and Stratton.

Wheldall, K. & Merret, F. (1984). *Positive Teaching: The Behavioural Approach*. London, Allan & Unwin.

Wilkins, D. (1979). *Caring for the Mentally Handicapped Child*. London, Croom Helm.

Woodhead, M. (1976). *Intervening in Disadvantage*. Slough, NFER.

Woods, G. (1981). 'Profiles: Parents help themselves'. *Child: Care, Health & Development*, 7, 51–56.

Woollams, S. & Brown, N. (1979). *The Total Handbook of Transactional Analysis*. New Jersey, Prentice-Hall.

Yule, W. and Carr, J. (1980). *Behaviour Modification for the Mentally Handicapped*. London, Croom Helm.

Index

171